A Yearbook of Seasons and Celebrations

To my dear Bogle nieces,
Isobel, Harriet, Iona, and Eleanor May
with much love

A Yearbook of
Seasons and Celebrations

Joanna Bogle

GRACEWING

AUSTRALIA

First published in 2007

Gracewing
2 Southern Avenue, Leominster
Herefordshire HR6 0QF

in Australia by:
Freedom Publishing Pty Ltd
582 Queensberry Street
North Melbourne
Victoria 3051

Special edition printed by arrangement with
Gracewing Publishing for:
✛ **Aid to the Church in Need**
12-14 Benhill Avenue, Sutton, Surrey SM1 4DA
Registered Charity No. 1097984

ISBN 978 0 85244 129 9

Cover image: *Bob Apple* by Frank Morgan (1856–1927).
Private collection/Photo © Rafael Valls Gallery, London, UK/
The Bridgeman Art Library.

Typesetting by Action Publishing Technology Ltd,
Gloucester, GL1 5SR

Printed in England by
Athenaeum Press Ltd, Gateshead NE11 0PZ

Contents

Contents

Contents

Acknowledgements

The quotations from the autobiography of Joseph Ratzinger, Pope Benedict XVI, are from *Milestones: Memoirs 1927–1977* (Ignatius Press, USA, 1998). The recipe for Greek Bean soup and the information on St John's Day in Christmastide are from *A Continual Feast: A Cookbook to celebrate the joys of family and faith throughout the Christian year* (Ignatius Press, USA, 1985), by Evelyn Birge Vitz, to whom I am also grateful for general advice and support. The source for the recipes for Lentil soup and for Vegetarian Loaf is *From a Benedictine Kitchen – Recipes from Minster Abbey*, published by the sisters at Minster-in-Thanet, Kent, with my thanks for their friendship. The honey-toffee recipe for St Bartholomew's Day is from *Festivals, Family and Food* by Diana Carey and Judy Large, a book which has provided me with much inspiration over the years. I am grateful to Canon Seamus Cunane, sometime parish priest of the Shrine of Our Lady of Cardigan for the information about Aberporth and the Assumption, and for his kind encouragement. My thanks go to my sister-in-law Dora Nash for the correct words and details on 'Auld Lang Syne', to my niece-in-law Fiorella Nash for information about customs and traditions in Malta, and to my Bogle sisters-in-law Jenny and Alison, for various cookery and other tips. My special thanks go to my own mother, Ursula Nash, and my mother-in-law, Susan Bogle, for a whole range of ideas and information as well as practical help.

Acknowledgements

Introduction

When my *Book of Feasts and Seasons* was first published in 1986, the idea was to revive interest in old festivals and customs which were in danger of being forgotten or abandoned in an age dominated by television and a consumer culture. There was also concern about the place of Christianity in a 'multicultural' Britain. All of these issues are still hugely relevant today, some twenty years later, and it seemed appropriate to supplement that original book with a new one, incorporating some of the fresh material gained during two decades of contacts made with church groups, schools, women's organizations and families. So this is a companion volume, and one which offers more information on saints' days and more ideas for things to make, eat, do, and sing around the whole year.

The arrival of the Internet has made it far easier to obtain information about feasts, festivals, customs, and traditions, and the vast array of foodstuffs now available in Britain's supermarkets makes cooking easy. But actually celebrating feasts – and fasts – takes organization, and a commitment to the idea that there are beliefs underpinning the way we live, and that ideals and values really do matter.

There is widespread concern that marriages and families today seem fragile – we have a very high divorce rate, and cohabitation outside marriage means even more fragmented and confused relationships. Church attendances continue to drop, and often Church spokesmen seem timid in the face of a public culture that is not merely indifferent to Christianity and its values but actively opposed to it.

This book is unashamedly Christian. It celebrates a culture based on the Faith around which our history has been written, through which we date our years and on which our legal system has been based for centuries. Future generations have a right to a knowledge of the songs, poems, legends, recipes, dances and stories associated with the round of Christian feasts and seasons. Those who think that Christianity is just a fable can still enjoy the rich traditions of

1

a culture which is two thousand years old and rooted in one far older. Those who deeply believe in another religious faith can enjoy the understanding that comes from a recognition that Christians do have a culture worth discovering, There are opportunities here for hospitality, friendship, and learning.

The Church's Seasons

Understanding the Christian year means obtaining the key to our calendar. Most people growing up in Britain will have some idea of what is meant by 'Christmas' and 'Easter' but only slightly hazy ideas about how they fit together. Some words, such as 'Pentecost' will be baffling to them. Increasingly the names of footballers and pop stars, and people acting in television soap operas, mean more to people's lives than the unfolding of the seasons and the culture that has shaped our lives and written our history. The year's round of seasons focuses on the need to have an expensive holiday somewhere very hot in the summer and to spend a lot of money on gifts and luxuries in December, and various other treats at regular intervals marking things like birthdays and anniversaries and people starting or leaving jobs.

How to start understanding the calendar? We need to start with some understanding of the Christian faith: a belief in God, and in his Son, Jesus Christ, who was born of the Virgin Mary, died on a cross on Calvary, rose from the dead and works today through his Church, seeking to bring everyone to an eternity of happiness in heaven.

For more than one and a half thousand years, the annual round of feasts and seasons in Britain has commemorated the great events in the life, death, and resurrection of Jesus Christ, and the life of the Church he founded with its saints and heroes. A great wealth of music and poetry, art, architecture, traditions, festivities, songs, prayers, recipes and more has grown up around all of this, and is still growing.

To understand the calendar is to grasp in a new way the huge significance of the Christian faith, and to understand the role that it continues to play in our common life.

The Nicene Creed

I believe in one God
the Father, the Almighty,
Maker of heaven and earth,
of all that is, seen and unseen.
I believe in one Lord, Jesus Christ,
the only Son of God,
eternally begotten of the Father,
God from God, Light from Light,
true God from true God,
begotten, not made,
of one Being with the Father.
Through him all things were made.
For us men and for our salvation
he came down from Heaven:
by the power of the Holy Spirit,
he became incarnate of the Virgin Mary,
and was made man.
For our sake he was crucified under Pontius Pilate;
he suffered death and was buried.
On the third day he rose again
in accordance with the Scriptures;
he ascended into Heaven
and is seated at the right hand of the Father.
He will come again in glory to judge the living and the dead,
and his kingdom will have no end.
I believe in the Holy Spirit, the Lord, the giver of life
who proceeds from the Father and the Son.
With the Father and the Son he is worshipped and glorified.
He has spoken through the Prophets.
I believe in one holy catholic and apostolic Church.
I acknowledge one baptism for the remission of sins
I look for the resurrection of the dead,
And the life of the world to come.
Amen.

How to understand the Calendar

Think of the year as a circle. It may help to draw one on a piece of paper. At the top, draw a small Christmas tree. That reminds us of Christmas, the annual feast that marks the birth of Jesus Christ. This feast is celebrated around the time of the winter solstice – that is to say, the shortest day of the year. Long ago our pagan ancestors understood some significance in the shortening and lengthening of the days. They sought to give some meaning to something that they could – correctly – see as symbolic of death and life, of endings and beginnings, perhaps even of some hint of life beyond the grave. The ancient Romans – whose religious ideas were in general more refined and coherent than those of the lands they conquered – also had feasts connected to the various seasons of the year.

Christ was born into the Roman Empire – that same Empire of which Britain was a part. As the story of his life, death, and resurrection, spread across the world – through the trade routes of the Empire – it was natural that a new and Christian significance would be given to the seasons of the year. At the time of the shortest and darkest day, it was natural to celebrate the birth of Christ, the 'Light of the World'. The Early Church, through much debate and also through practical experience, found itself 'inculturating' itself into the customs and traditions of people everywhere. It also had its rich Jewish tradition and background, in which dates and seasons were of central importance and in which the timing of the Passover was deeply connected to the great Christian 'new Passover' of Christ, the ultimate Paschal Lamb, sacrificed once and for all so that all of humanity could 'pass over' into union with God and a share in his blessings. The old pagan beliefs represent some sort of hope in a Divinity: now, in Christ, God himself reaches down to answer, and to make sense of the longing placed in people's hearts and expressed through pagan religions.

Draw a straight line down from your Christmas tree to the bottom of the circle. That's Midsummer Day, the summer solstice, the longest day of the year. In the Church calendar, 24 June – the summer equivalent of 24 December, Christmas Eve – is the 'summer Christmas', the feast of the birthday of John the Baptist.

John the Baptist links the Old and the New Testaments. You will read more about him in the section of this book devoted to June – but it is important to understand his prophetic role, as the cousin

5

of Christ who prepared the way for the coming of the Saviour. He said of Christ, 'He must increase and I must decrease': after John the Baptist's birthday, the days get shorter, after Christ's they get longer.

Now draw a line right across the circle, intersecting the vertical one. You now have a circle with a big cross over it. It all looks a bit like a hot cross bun! That's not accidental. The hot cross bun, which we traditionally eat on Good Friday – a round spicy bun with a cross made of light pastry on it – is meant to remind us of the Crucifixion of Christ. It is also a symbol of the year, divided into four quarters: spring, summer, autumn, and winter, all dominated by the cross. The bun also represents the world – which is of course round – under the rule of Christ.

This is, incidentally, the same image that is represented by the orb, the round gleaming sphere made of silver and gold and topped by an ornate cross, that the Queen was given at her coronation, and which every monarch has been given at every coronation down the centuries in our country. It is an ancient symbol of Christian kingship – the earth under the dominion of the Cross. (It also reminds us that our ancestors certainly didn't think that the earth was flat – they knew perfectly well that it was round, and always depicted it as such.)

Back to our image of the year. Where the horizontal line meets the circle, you can mark the spring equinox (equal hours of day and night) on the right and the autumnal equinox on the left. The spring equinox, in March, is honoured by the Church as 'Lady Day' or the feast of the Annunciation, the day when the Virgin Mary learned from the Angel Gabriel that she was to have a child, who would be the world's Saviour. Count it up: from 25 March to 25 December is exactly nine months, the time spent by a child in the womb of his mother, until he is ready to be born.

In the 'spring' section of your circle – upper right-hand section – you can write 'Lent/Holy Week/Easter'. This is Paschal-tide, the time of the Passover.

You now have the basics of the Christian calendar, centred on the events of the life of Christ as described in the Scriptures. But there is more – much more. Into this circular framework we must now fit the drama of the Christian year: Ascension and Pentecost as the Easter story completes itself, then Advent as a preparation for Christmas, and the whole Christmas season itself with Epiphany and Candlemas. Then there are the saints' days – a saint's feast-day

6

is the day on which he or she died, and the tradition of commemorating them goes right back to the Early Church and the martyrs
who died for the Christian faith in pagan Rome. And as there will
always be new saints and new adventures to commemorate, this
calendar is always changing, especially as in addition to the general
Christian calendar – used worldwide having originated in the
Middle East and Europe in the Church's earliest days – there are
adaptions for the local calendars of different nations and peoples.

Living the calendar, celebrating its feasts, enjoying the ways in
which they mesh with the natural seasons of the year, gives a new
appreciation of the gift of life itself and of our relationship both
with the natural world and with the customs and culture that we
have inherited. It enables us to see things in perspective – we
understand that history has gone before us, and that we can and
should be doing useful and great things with the days that are given
to us.

Christianity has always had a deep understanding of time. Every
day and hour and moment is precious. Jesus Christ was born into
human time, and therefore sanctified it. The Scriptures speak a
great deal of time – of God's ordering of the world, of time as being
of importance to him, with one day set aside each week on which
we should worship him. The monks, whose monasteries and abbeys
across Europe created European culture, were the first to give
human beings a sense of structured and ordered time – with eight
hours daily of work, eight of rest, and eight of prayer.

Advent

God prepared for the coming of his Son over the centuries. He awakened in the hearts of the pagans a dim expectation of this coming and he prepared for it specifically through the Old Testament, culminating with John the Baptist who was the last and greatest of the prophets. We relive this long period of expectancy in the annual liturgical celebration of the season of Advent.

Compendium of the Catechism of the Catholic Church, 2006

In the Creed, Christians speak of their belief in God, and in his Son, Jesus Christ: 'For us men and for our salvation he came down from Heaven: by the power of the Holy Spirit, he was born of the Virgin Mary, and became man.' The birth of Jesus Christ is celebrated at Christmas, and thus the Church's year begins with Advent, the four weeks of preparation leading up to the great Christmas feast.

The word 'advent' means 'coming'. We are looking forward to the coming of Christ at Christmas.

The first Sunday of Advent is traditionally known as 'Stir up Sunday' because of the prayer used in church, beginning 'Stir up we beseech thee, O Lord . . .' It asked God to stir up our hearts with love for him, but people also took it as a reminder to stir up the Christmas puddings.

A good Christmas pudding should be made several weeks before Christmas, and 'Stir Up Sunday' is a good day to make it. Every standard cookery book will have a recipe: many families have their own, handed down from one generation to the next. Some families make two, and enjoy one of them at Christmas and the other at Easter: with plenty of alcohol in it, a Christmas pudding should keep for a good while.

It is traditional for every member of the household to take a turn at stirring the Christmas pudding, closing the eyes and making a secret wish while stirring. The mixture can be kept in the bowl, covered with a clean cloth, until everyone has had a turn; keeping it standing for a few hours is said to improve the flavour.

Christmas Pudding

4 oz each of:
Currants
Raisins
Sultanas
Mixed peel

A glass (say 5 tablespoons) of brandy or sherry
Juice and grated rind of 1 lemon
6 oz butter
2 eggs
8 oz demerara sugar
8 oz fresh breadcrumbs
4 oz self-raising flour
1 dessertspoonful of mixed spice
One teaspoonful of grated nutmeg

Cream together the butter and sugar, then add the eggs and beat well. Add all the remaining ingredients and stir very well until you have a rich, smooth mixture. If the mixture seems dry, add some orange juice, milk or beer.

Pack the mixture into a good-sized pudding basin, and cover with a sheet of greaseproof paper and silver foil. A square of linen cloth (e.g. an old table napkin) over all this is useful too. Secure all this firmly with string. Stand the pudding basin in a large saucepan of water and bring it to the boil, and steam it for 4 hours. Do not let it boil dry!

On Christmas Day itself, you will need to steam this pudding for a further 2 hours. It should emerge dark and moist.

Bestir thy power, Lord, we pray thee, and come! Be thou our protec-
tor and deliverer. So may we be found worthy to be rescued from the
judgement that threatens us by reason of our sins.
            old version of the Collect for the First Sunday of Advent

Marking the Season of Advent

'*The people that walked in darkness have seen a great light*' (Isaiah).

O come O come Emmanuel,
And ransom captive Israel,
That mourns in lonely exile here,
Until the Son of God appear,
Rejoice! Rejoice!
Emmanuel
Shall come to thee, O Israel.

O come thou Rod of Jesse free
Thine own from Satan's tyranny;
From depths of Hell they people save,
And give them victory o'er the grave.
Rejoice! etc.

O come thou Dayspring, come and cheer
Our spirits by thine advent here;
Disperse the gloomy clouds of night,
And death's dark shadows put to flight.
Rejoice! etc.

O come thou Key of David, come,
And open wide our heavenly home;
Make safe the way that leads on high,
And close the path to misery.
Rejoice! etc.

O come O come thou Lord of might
Who to thy tribes, on Sinai's height,
In ancient times didst give the law
In cloud, and majesty and awe.
Rejoice! etc.

Veni, veni Emmanuel
Based on the Advent 'O' antiphons
Tr John Mason Neale 1818–1866

The four Sundays of Advent can be a special time, as Christmas draws nearer and excitement builds. But it takes a special effort to keep commercial pressures at bay and foster the real meaning of this time.

10

The Advent Wreath

An Advent wreath can be the focus of family devotion at this time. This very delightful custom is relatively new in Britain – it only arrived in the 1920s and was popularized in the 1960s via the children's television programme 'Blue Peter' – but it has been part of life in German-speaking countries for generations.

Essentially, an Advent wreath is a large circle of evergreens, into which are fixed four stout candles, one for each of the Sundays of Advent. Probably, the frame for the wreath would originally have been a cartwheel, when on country farms in Austria and Germany, the wheels of a cart would be removed in winter for repairs: a sleigh was more useful in the snowy weather. Today, a firm base for a wreath can be three or four coils of thick wire, round which you then firmly bind the greenery. The candles can also be attached by wire: coil it carefully round the base of each candle up to about two or three inches.

Traditionally the four candles are red, and the wreath is decorated with red ribbons. It can be hung up from the ceiling, rather like a candelabra or an old-fashioned kitchen lantern hanging from the rafters. But this is problematical in a modern house, and its best place is probably the centre of the kitchen table. One candle is lit for the first Sunday of Advent, two for the second, and so on.

The traditional liturgical colour for Advent is purple: the priest will wear purple vestments at Mass and there will be purple altar hangings in church. So purple candles and ribbons are also appropriate for the Advent wreath. One idea for the Advent wreath is to have three purple candles, and one pink one, for the third Sunday – of which more in a moment.

The Advent wreath isn't just meant to be a decoration. It is a focus for family prayers. It can be lit during the family evening meal, when Grace is said. Or it can be lit on a Sunday evening, and perhaps a verse of an Advent carol sung, with everyone then joining in the 'Our Father'.

One big advantage of having an Advent wreath is that it takes the pressure off putting up the Christmas tree too early. With a large and beautiful wreath, replete with candles and ribbons (in our family, we also add some tinsel and other decorations), we don't need a tree just yet, and we can enjoy every moment of this season as Christmas draws nearer and nearer.

11

Gaudete Sunday

Advent is a season of penance in preparation for Christmas: a time to go to confession, and to make an effort to spend extra time in prayer. It is meant to be a time when we really prepare our hearts for the great message of Christmas, reminding ourselves that Christ came to live among us and be our Saviour. On the third Sunday of Advent, Gaudete Sunday, the solemn mood is lifted: Christmas is really near now. The purple vestments give way to rose-coloured ones, and there is a mood of joy in the liturgy at Mass. The Latin word *Gaudete* gives us words like 'gaudy' and indicates celebration and joyfulness (at Oxford University, a celebration dinner-night is known as a 'gaudy').

Gaudete Sunday could be a good day for putting up the Christmas crib, and perhaps for putting a Christmassy wreath on the front door. It can mark the start of the carol-singing season (we could choose one to sing as we light the pink/rose-coloured candle on the Advent wreath), and we could bake the first batch of mince pies.

> *Rejoice in the Lord always*
> *And again I say to you rejoice.* (Ps. 84)

A Christmas Crib

Every family should have a Nativity scene: it is now possible to buy extremely attractive crib figures, and it is worth investing in this when the children are small. Look in gift-shops at churches and cathedrals, or browse advertisements in Catholic magazines and newspapers for mail-order possibilities, or look at the range of beautiful Nativity sets available via the Internet. St Francis of Assisi is said to have created the first crib scene, as a way of teaching people how to visualize the scene in that stable in Bethlehem when Christ was born: Italy is still famous for its beautiful Nativity scenes, and a massive one is erected every year in St Peter's Square, floodlit at night, and visited by the Pope.

A stable/cave can be made out of papier-mâché: tear up pieces of newspaper into small pieces, put these in a bucket with hot water, and stir this around into a mushy pulp. Then add about a quarter of a packet of wallpaper paste (obtainable from any do-it-yourself shop). Stir this about a good deal, and you now have a good paper pulp which is ideal for modelling.

You can make a cave by putting lots papier-mâché over crunched-up chicken wire, or you can use a cardboard box as a base and build a cave-scene around it. You dry the whole thing out by putting it somewhere warm overnight. Then paint it brown or grey, and if you want it to look snowy, cover it with tinsel and glitter and cotton wool. It is now ready to receive Mary and Joseph, the shepherds, an angel or two, and – at Epiphany – the Three Kings with their camels and gifts.

A Nativity scene is a lovely present for a grandparent or god-parent to give to a family. Extras can be added year by year: a proper stable, some extra angels, candles in good-quality candle-sticks to stand on either side.

When erecting the crib, choose where it will be placed. On a table somewhere central? In the hall? On a mantelpiece in the main room? It should be somewhere that can be a focus for prayer, and also where the scene can be enjoyed and admired. It is nice to have at least one candle burning there in the evenings.

It is traditional to leave the manger empty, and to place the Christ-child there after Midnight Mass on Christmas Eve (keep him somewhere safe in the meantime!). Another tradition is to have the Three Magi waiting some distance away, perhaps even in another room – they can make their way slowly, day by day, towards Bethlehem, across the tops of shelves and perhaps even down the stairs having first visited each of the children's rooms: moving them each day becomes part of Advent.

> In the fields in the autumn we looked for wild lettuce, and by the Salzach in the meadows Mother showed us now to find many useful things for our nativity scene, of which we were particularly fond. One of my most delightful memories is the visit we would make around Christmas time to an elderly lady whose nativity scene almost filled the whole of her living room and had so many wonderful things in it that you could not contemplate it long enough.
> Cardinal Joseph Ratzinger, now Pope Benedict XVI, *Milestones*.

The Christmas Tree and St Boniface

Bringing greenery into the house at Christmas time has origins that go back into the distant mists of pagan history – the idea that evergreen branches, which do not die when everything else does in winter, are a pledge of life beyond death, and of survival through winter until spring. Christians were able to adapt such notions easily to the Christian idea. The Christmas tree can be associated with all sorts of useful Christian imagery – the Tree of Life, the Jesse Tree from the Old Testament, and the Tree of Calvary on which Christ died.

Tradition says that an English missionary saint, St Boniface – born Wynfrith at Crediton in Devon – created the first authentic Christmas tree, in Germany. The pagan Germanic tribes worshipped trees, and in order to impress on them that they must worship God – the creator of the trees – rather than the trees themselves, Boniface felled a conifer. Nothing terrible happened: no disaster or horror occurred, and Boniface took the tree indoors and decorated it with lights, teaching about Christ as the Light of the World.

Boniface, born in 675, is not much honoured in his native Britain, but is revered in Germany. He became a monk at Nursling near Southampton, taking the name Boniface (from the Latin *bonus* meaning 'good' and *facere* 'to do' – i.e. one who seeks to do good) and later went to Germany where he worked as a vigorous missionary, travelling to Hesse, Bavaria, Westphalia and Thuringia. He went to Rome three times to report progress, and was responsible for establishing the Church firmly among the German-speaking peoples. He was made bishop in 732, establishing his see at Mainz, and finally met his death by martyrdom. His tomb at Fulda, where he had founded a monastery, is much visited by pilgrims today.

The story of St Boniface ought to be part of our Christmas folklore. His feast-day is on 5 June, but why not honour him among the Christmas saints, and tell his story as the family Christmas tree is erected and its lights and decorations enjoyed?

Saints and Feast-Days in Advent

The various saints' days that fall during Advent play a vital part in establishing the culture of the season. The most important is St Nicholas or Santa Claus, who has come down to us in today's culture as 'Father Christmas'. But there are a number of others, and marking each of their days makes the whole of December into something memorable and special – and stops us celebrating Christmas before we should.

St Barbara: 4 December

Patron saint of fireworks, of thunder, and of artillery regiments, St Barbara has long been hailed as a popular saint and martyr. Little is really known about her but she is said to have been a young Christian woman in the early years of the Church, in the pagan Roman Empire, whose pagan father wanted a brilliant marriage for her, but she wanted to dedicate her life to Christ. In a fit of anger, her family denounced her to the authorities and her father was himself ordered to execute her. As his sword swooped down severing her head from her body, he was himself struck dead by a bolt of lightning. The site of her martyrdom has variously been given as Tuscany, Rome, and Egypt, and the date is usually during the Diocletian persecution, i.e. about the year AD 300. The legend of the thunderbolt striking her father has linked her to fireworks, and having some fireworks today is a traditional way to celebrate her feast-day. She is invoked, of course, against danger from storms, and is the patron of artillery regiments in a number of countries – again because of the link with fireworks and explosives generally. She is also the patron saint of miners, and in some parts of Europe they used to hang special candle-lanterns at the mines in her honour on her feast-day.

St Nicholas: 6 December

This great bishop of the fourth century has become a major part of Christmas for millions, simply because he happened to die in December and thus acquire a feast-day in the run-up to Christmastide. He was Bishop of Myra, and was among those who took part in the great Church Council at Nicaea which gave us the Nicene Creed, which we still say every Sunday at Mass. This Creed specifically emphasizes the Trinity: God as Father, Son, and Holy Ghost. St Nicholas was a great teacher of the Trinity, emphasizing that Jesus Christ is truly God (against the Arian heresy – which has been revived in our own day – which taught that he was simply a very good and kind man with no claim to divinity). Because of this link with the Trinity, stories about St Nicholas tend to emphasize the number three.

Bishop Nicholas had a great concern for the welfare of the young, especially their moral welfare. Learning of a family of three orphan girls, who were reduced to thinking of prostitution in order to survive, he is said to have thrown small bags of money down the chimney for them to find in the fireplace. This is the origin of the idea that 'Santa Claus comes down the chimney' with gifts, and also of the idea that charitable giving at Christmas should be done generously and discreetly: helping needy families should never be carried out in such a way as to embarrass them. The three bags of money are still commemorated in the small mesh bags of chocolate golden coins that children find in their stockings from Father Christmas. They are also commemorated in the traditional sign for a pawnbroker: three round brass balls. You will sometimes today see this sign outside a wine bar – often it means that the building was originally a pawnbroker, where people could take their jewellery or other items, and 'pawn' them for money, getting them back when they were in funds again.

In Holland, Belgium, Austria, Germany, and elsewhere, the arrival of St Nicholas is a major event for many families. He may arrive in style, as a major community event, dressed as an elderly bishop with a splendid white beard, a mitre, crozier, and cope. Sometimes he comes as part of a parade through the town, or he may simply come to a church hall or a children's hospital. Either way, he brings sweets, tangerines, apples and chocolate coins, and small toys, and – in theory anyway – he has a big book in which the children's good and bad deeds are said to be listed. Sometimes he has a scary figure with him – *Schwarz Peter* or *Rupprecht* (it varies), who rattles chains and will take away with him any children deemed to have been badly-behaved during the year.

It might be possible for St Nicholas to arrive at your home, and it is a wonderful way to have a celebration. A mitre can be made from cardboard – with two strips of material hanging down the back (look up some pictures of bishops to get this right) – and a crozier from a suitably decorated walking stick; a curtain might serve as a cope. St Nicholas should have a sack with sweets, biscuits, apples, chocolate coins etc. in it – and a stick or a ruler which he passes solemnly to parents with instructions to use it if necessary on any naughty children. The largest book you can find (encyclopedia? Bible?), covered with white paper and with a big label saying something like

'CHILDREN'S DEEDS' and the date of the year, completes his equipment. He might just bless all the children and leave the sweets – or he might decide to ask everyone if they've been good, and go through a great show of checking in his book . . . and the children might sing some carols for him. *Lebkuchen* cakes and spiced *Bischopswyn* (Bishop's wine) could be served.

Another way for St Nicholas to arrive is secretly. Sometimes a knock is heard at the front door and when it is opened, no one is there but sweets and small toys are left on the mat. More usually, shoes – well-polished for the occasion – are left by the fireplace on the Eve of St Nicholas and in the morning these are found to be filled with goodies. In this case, a bottle of beer for St Nicholas, and carrots for his donkey, should be left along with the shoes. Letters are sometimes written from children, making a promise about being good and celebrating Christmas in a proper spirit.

It seems a pity just to let all this happen without the children learning something about St Nicholas and his message: there really is meant to be a genuine spiritual side to the celebration. St Nicholas was a confessor – even as 'Father Christmas' he has come down to us in folklore as someone who knows our good and bad deeds and who wants us to learn to be good. Today, commercialism has overtaken the older version of his feast-day, which had children actually kneeling down in front of him and receiving a blessing along with their gifts – something of this can be revived by telling the story of his life (there is plenty on the Internet about him, just tap 'St Nicholas' into any search engine, and any good library will also have a book of saints in which he will be found, as will any Christian bookshop).

The arrival of St Nicholas on his feast-day doesn't mean that he can't come again on Christmas Eve to fill stockings – family traditions can accommodate a whole range of things!

The red robes of 'Santa Claus' or 'Father Christmas' were originally a bishop's robes. The American image of 'Santa Claus' that we have today – the tubby figure in red trousers and fur-trimmed jacket – began in the 1930s when it was used in advertising. In its earlier versions, the idea of Santa Claus fitted in with a folklore tradition of a winter figure who was depicted as an old man – contrasting with springtime, seen as a young girl.

There used to be a tradition – still occasionally revived – of choirboys electing one of their number as a 'boy bishop' on St Nicholas Day. The boy was given a miniature set of bishop's robes, and presided at ceremonies – it was a way of teaching the choirboys about correct liturgy and ceremonial. The 'boy bishop' held office until Holy Innocents' Day (28 December), which was a holiday with games and treats after all the hard work of singing at the great ceremonies over Christmas.

> *O good St Nicholas*
> *Who brings joy to children*
> *Put into my heart the spirit of childhood*
> *Of which the Gospel speaks*
> *And teach me to sow happiness around me*
> *You, whose feast prepares us for Christmas*
> *Open my faith to the mystery of God made man.*
> (French prayer to St Nicholas. Anon)

Lebkuchen

(German honey cakes for St Nicholas Day)

    8 oz self-raising flour
    1/2 teaspoon of ground cloves
    1/2 teaspoon of mixed spice
    1/2 teaspoon of ground cinnamon
    5 oz honey
    9 oz golden syrup
    3 oz sugar
    1 oz butter
    Greaseproof paper; baking tray

Heat the oven to Gas Mark 6 (400°F). Mix the flour and all the spices together in a bowl. In a saucepan, heat the honey, golden syrup and sugar, stirring until all the sugar is dissolved. Remove and add the butter, stirring until it is melted. Now add the flour mixture, about 4 oz at a time. When the batter mixture is smooth, drop it on to greased sheets of paper. Bake for about 10 minutes. Remove the cakes carefully and cool them on a cake-rack. When they are cool, glaze them: stir about 2 oz of icing sugar into cold water, with a teaspoon of lemon juice and some almond essence. Stir until it is smooth and the spread this on the cakes. Another idea is to dip the cakes into melted chocolate.

Bischopswyn (Dutch-style spiced wine)

1 orange with cloves stuck into it (children enjoy doing this)
1 cinnamon stick
Peel of 1 lemon
Bottle of red wine
Sugar

Put the orange studded with the cloves into the wine – this is best done some hours before. Then heat the wine with all the other ingredients. The amount of sugar is up to personal taste.

The Immaculate Conception: 8 December

'Hail, full of grace' (Luke 1:28). The Angel's greeting to Mary has become familiar to us. But it is a strange greeting. How can an ordinary human being be described as 'full of grace'? Only through the saving grace of God – whom Mary herself later described as her Saviour, in that great prayer the Magnificat, in which she says that 'the Almighty has done great things for me – holy is his name'. Yet this was before Christ's death on Calvary. Her case was exceptional: God, who is author of all time, saved her from sin at a moment of his own choosing, through the same Saviour that he used for everyone else but in a unique way. On 8 December the Catholic Church celebrates the 'great things' that God did for Mary, saving her from sin through the merits of the Cross, so that she was free from sin from the moment of her conception, and thus a fitting mother for the Redeemer. Note that this feast-day is exactly nine months before the feast of Mary's Birthday on 8 September. Note too, that it refers to Mary's conception – i.e. that she was sinless from the moment she was first created. This is something different from Christ's virginal conception in Mary's womb – which we honour at the Annunciation in March – and his birth, which we will honour soon at Christmas.

> O purest of creatures, sweet mother, sweet maid
> The one spotless womb in which Jesus was laid.

St Lucy: 13 December

St Lucy, although a native of Italy, is much honoured in Scandinavia. It is possible that Vikings learned about her on their travels and took the message home. In Sweden and Denmark, there is very little daylight at this time of year. The name Lucy means 'light' – it is the same Latin root which gives us words like 'lucid' and 'translucent'. A saint whose name evokes light is just right for December.

St Lucy's name is mentioned in the Canon of the Mass: she is one of a number of early Christian martyrs who were young girls. She died in the great persecution under the Emperor Diocletian and her date of death is usually given at approximately 304, which means she belongs to the same era as St Barbara and St Nicholas. She wanted to dedicate her whole life to God and remain a virgin, and was martyred because she refused to renounce this. At one point she was forcibly locked up in a brothel. She is said to have been finally martyred by a sword thrust to her throat.

In Scandinavia, the daughter in a family becomes the *Lussibrud* or 'St Lucy Bride' on *Luciadagen*, or St Lucy's Day. She is supposed to rise very early and – wearing a crown of candles and greenery, and a long white dress with a wide red ribbon sash – to serve fresh coffee and saffron buns to everyone! But often the celebration takes place at teatime, and St Lucia – with her long fair hair hanging loose and her white dress giving her the look of a Christmas angel – entertains her friends to a feast. Cakes and pastries are also taken to old people's homes, and school groups led by a *Lussibrud* – the candle-crown can be made with pretend candles made out of cardboard, although there are also battery-operated versions which give real light! – go there to sing carols and distribute small gifts. The traditional cakes for St Lucy's Day are *Lussekattor* – Lucy's cats – which are saffron pastries.

This could be a wonderful day for little girls to enjoy, and it is beginning to become popular in America. A florist's shop may have the basis for a St Lucy crown with a wreath of greenery into which you could put some candles, though probably something artificial is best! A trawl through the Internet will give recipes for saffron buns and Danish pastries, as will any cookery book that offers recipes from Sweden or Denmark.

It seems possible that part of the St Lucy legend dates back to a time of great famine in Scandinavia: when ships bringing grain finally arrived girls hurried from farm to farm in the early morning, while it was still dark, with the food. There is also an Italian tradition associated with St Lucy: in a time of famine, people begged her prayers for help, and a ship miraculously arrived with a large quantity of grain. The people were so hungry that they simply boiled it and ate it as a sort of porridge, without bothering to mill it into flour to make bread. A form of porridge (*cuccia*) is still eaten in Palermo on St Lucy's Day.

It is this story, too, which has given rise to the tradition of St Lucy's wheat: you plant some grains of wheat on St Lucy's Day in a pot of moist soil. Keep it all watered – not too soggy – and the wheat will sprout, and there will be a nice display of greenery by Christmas Day. Tie a ribbon round the pot and it all forms part of your Christmas decorations.

Today, the whole idea of a virgin martyr, and indeed any celebration for girls that focuses on something pretty, innocent and feminine, is likely to be regarded as hopelessly old-fashioned – which is a very good reason for doing it!

Because of the association with light, St Lucy is invoked for diseases of the eyes. She is also of course the patron of St Lucia, in the West Indies.

> Night falls, its darkness dread
> Rich and poor steeping
> From earth the sun is fled
> Shadows are creeping
> When to a darkened world
> Comes with new light unfurled
> *Santa Lucia, Santa Lucia*
>
> Hope glimmers through the gloom
> New life is stirring
> In every silent room
> Soft as wings whirring.
> L o'er the threshold bright
> White-robed with candle-light
> *Santa Lucia, Santa Lucia*

Preparing for Christmas

The final days before Christmas are always busy ones, and a major problem today is that Christmas carol services and school Nativity

21

plays start in November, so people are really almost tired of Christmas by the time it actually arrives. (Can't some schools and parishes start having ADVENT events instead? It's so inappropriate to have Christmas celebrations when it's not yet Christmas, and something advertised as an Advent Carol Service could surely work well?).

But this shouldn't mean that real preparation for Christmas gets ignored. Of course there is all the fuss with the practicalities of family Christmas arrangements – travel, presents, meals, hospitality, all inevitably made complicated by the tangles of family relationships ... but in the end the real meaning of Christmas is too important to be allowed to be lost. So in the final days before Christmas there's still time to:

> – Get to confession at church: find out times of confession in the local church, or in some city church or cathedral which could be visited during a shopping trip.
> – Check times of Christmas Masses and services (NOTE: in some country districts, Midnight Mass may not be at midnight!)
> – Make sure we've given to some worthwhile charity.

Making Christmas biscuits and mince pies is fun and gives the house a nice smell in the run-up to Christmas! Mincemeat consists of raisins, currants, and other dried fruit, plus chopped apples, spices, orange juice, lemon juice, and lots of alcohol – and shredded suet. This last is an echo of the days when the essence of the dish was minced-up meat itself, dried or salted meat, preserved for the winter and normally rather dreary to eat, but spiced up with all these tasty extras. Mince pies are made of sweetened shortcrust pastry and are traditionally small and oval in shape – to commemorate the manger at Bethlehem, with Christ as the sweetness inside. Some say that the traditional crimped edges represent the hills and dales over which Mary and Joseph travelled as they made their way to Bethlehem for the census. The name 'manger', incidentally, seems to be significant: think of the French word for 'to eat' – the infant Christ being placed in the animals' feeding-trough, where the grain would be placed on which they fed, has a Eucharistic message: he is the Bread of Life and even his birth gives us a foretelling of Holy Communion ...

Carol Singing

An evening of carol singing is well worth the effort. You don't need official permission or any kind of licence to go from house to house singing carols and collecting for charity. Gather together some friends, fix a date, and get in some hymn books (borrow from church or school). Start people off with a glass of spiced wine and try out a couple of carols at home. Use the old favourites: 'O come O come Emmanuel', 'Away in a Manger', 'O come all ye faithful' (this works extremely well in Latin too: '*Adeste Fideles*'), 'While shepherds watched', 'We Three Kings'. Then go on your way. A lantern tied to a stick looks nice with the group. Have a proper collecting box or jam jar with a label on it giving the name of the charity for which you are collecting, and a leaflet or two in case anyone asks for details.

To sing at a railway station or some other public place – unless it is directly outside a church and on church property – you will almost certainly need permission. Contact local police, the local council, or railway or other transport authorities. If you want to sing at a main railway station or other popular place, PERMISSION MAY NEED TO BE SOUGHT SOME MONTHS IN ADVANCE!

A Gingerbread House

A little house, made entirely out of gingerbread, representing the house in the 'Hansel and Gretel' fairy story, is another Christmas tradition, and is something that is fun to make. It is possible to buy special kits that make up into these houses, but you can also simply make two trays of gingerbread, and build a house yourself. The four sides are stuck together with icing, and you can use sweets and pieces of chocolate (stuck on with icing) to create windows – complete with window boxes in the German style – a doorway, and additions like a water butt, and a garden path and gate. Although the sloping roof is meant to be made of gingerbread, too, you can cheat and simply make this of a large piece of folded white cardboard, with plenty of glitter and tinsel to represent snow.

23

What Gifts to Buy?

'Children today have everything!' is the cry heard from many grandparents – and it certainly is true that many children seem to have shelves and shelves of plastic toys, often unappreciated and rarely touched. What can a grandparent or godparent give to a child who seems glutted with everything?

One idea is simply: books. Every child should have access to the great children's classics. At the end of this book is a list – drawn up after consultation with lots of friends and relations – of books that we believe should form part of the childhood of every child in the English-speaking world. A book is the ideal Christmas present, and it means that you can keep in touch with the child, talk about what he or she is reading, and have something that you share together.

And it is not just children from comfortable homes that need books. They are the birthright of every child in the world. The international Catholic charity Aid to the Church in Need (1, Times Square, Sutton, Surrey SM1) has published a delightful Child's Bible, which has been translated into the many languages of every continent on earth. Already, millions of this attractive, brightly illustrated book have been distributed: to children in war-torn Africa and in the shanty towns of Latin America, to children for whom it may be the only book they ever actually own throughout their childhood years, to children who have no access to the large bookshops and well-stocked libraries of today's British and American youngsters. If you donate to Aid to the Church in Need, at Christmas, the same sum that you spend on a grandchild or godchild, and ask that it goes to the Children's Bible Project, you will have done something worthwhile, and enabled a child to have real pleasure and a feast of good reading.

Mince Pies

For shortcrust pastry:

8 oz flour
4 oz butter
A little milk
Flour for kneading and rolling
Sugar to sprinkle

Mincemeat:
Either buy a jar of ready-made mincemeat (plenty on sale at this time of year) or make your own by mixing together:

    4 oz each of raisins, currants, and sultanas
    Three chopped raw peeled apples,
    2 oz shredded suet
    Grated rind of 1 lemon and 1 orange, and the juice of each
    1 packet of glacé cherries
    Chopped mixed peel

These should ideally be put through an old-fashioned mincing machine, but if you don't have one of those, just chop everything up finely. Then add:

    1/2 teaspoonful of mixed spice
    1/2 teaspoonful of grated nutmeg
    A glass of brandy
    A splash of sweet sherry
    2 oz granulated sugar

Place this mixture into clean jam jars, and cover these tightly with a film of plastic (circles cut from a clean plastic bag, and held in place with a rubber band, will work well). It should keep for some while, and be useful for several batches of pies.

Pastry
Chop the butter into small pieces and then work it into the flour with your finger until the mixture resembles breadcrumbs. Then mix this into a paste with the milk – don't let it get too sticky! Knead it carefully on a floured board. Toss some flour over the rolling pin and roll out the pastry, then cut it into circles with a crinkle-edged pastry-cutter, some circles about 1½ inches in diameter, and some smaller.

Put the larger circles into well greased patty-pans, and a spoonful of mincemeat in each, then top these with the smaller circles. Press down gently to close each pie. Brush a little milk on top of each pie. Bake in a moderate oven for about 20 minutes. Dust generously with sugar before serving with whipped cream.

Christmas Decorations

The holly bears a berry
As red as any blood
And Mary bore sweet Jesus Christ
To do poor sinners good
                    Old carol

Evergreens are the traditional Christmas decorations: they are a symbol of the eternal life that Christ offers to us. The medieval understanding of Christmas was very much linked to the message of the Cross and Resurrection: hence older carols tend to mention this – the blood of Christ, shed for us (foretold, in a sense, by the massacre of the Innocents by Herod), the bittersweet idea that this baby would, as a man, bring salvation and joy through his suffering. Rosemary – the herb is named after Christ's mother – makes an attractive addition to other evergreens with its pleasing minty scent and sprigs of it, along with holly, can be tucked up behind pictures.

Christmas cards can be hung on cotton strung across the ceiling – this gets them out of the way and they look cheery. The purple candles and ribbons on the Advent wreath can be replaced with red as Christmas draws near, and the greenery renewed with perhaps some baubles and Christmas tree ornaments added too.

The tree itself should go up last – some families still stick to the rule that it should only arrive on Christmas Eve, others allow a few days earlier. One family started the tradition of putting it up just a few days before Christmas and adding a few ornaments every evening, as part of the gradual build-up which also included prayers round the Advent wreath. It is nice to put attractively-wrapped presents under the tree as they arrive, rather than hiding them away – but there must be a strict 'no-poking' rule so this probably only works for families with older children.

Depending on what you are buying for Christmas presents, it is also a good idea to make sure that the household has at least one good board game and/or a jigsaw for Christmas afternoon – remember these are good presents for older people, as well as for children, especially if the jigsaw is a really good one or relates to a place that has been visited and enjoyed during the year.

Christmas

Bittersweet?

This idea that Christmas is bittersweet – that Christ's suffering is foretold by the massacre of the Innocents, that the holly's sharp thorn already points us to the Crown of Thorns – is surely something that in its own way brings comfort at Christmas. For there is nothing more depressing than to be told to be merry and happy when in fact you have good reason to be sorrowful. Christmas is a difficult time for many people: for those recently bereaved, for the divorced – especially those separated from their children – for divided families, for the lonely, for those in prison (especially if unjustly, but also even if deservedly), for families struggling with someone mentally or physically ill. We can do something about some of these – in the days before Christmas it's important to think about neighbours who may be alone and who could be invited to Christmas lunch or tea, or could have a visit on Christmas afternoon with a gift. But for some sorrows there is no immediate relief, and the only real consolation is in the literal truth of the Christmas message. It's honestly not about expensive presents and food and lots of alcohol, or even about sentimental images of a baby lying on hay. It's about our redemption, and this was bought at a price which involved suffering – a God who truly understands all human unhappiness because he has been there too.

Christmas Eve

Then finally we are at Christmas Eve. This is the Holy Night celebrated in carols. Country folklore used to say that cattle in the cowsheds knelt at midnight on this night to honour the hour of the birth of the Saviour. For hundreds of years, all across Europe, the church bells have rung out and people have gone to church at midnight. In the days when Communism was meant to have replaced the Christian religion across half of Europe with a militant atheism, the Christian faith was alive in millions of hearts and homes, and people still believed. It is still alive today, although threatened by massive commercial pressures and by the dictates of a semi-official secular ideology. Christmas is a time to rediscover this faith if it has become marginal to our lives ...

The British tradition is to have the main celebrations on Christmas morning, but with increasing travel to mainland Europe, we are beginning to rediscover Christmas Eve.

The tradition is not to eat any meat on Christmas Eve – a link back to the days when fasting and abstinence was observed on this day as part of the penitential Advent season. So the main dish is fish – usually carp. The meal, being in the evening, is candlelit and traditionally seems to have had a more religious feel than the jollifications of paper hats and crackers that are part of the next day's British Christmas dinner. Of course in the past it concluded with a general departure for Midnight Mass – and that's still the crucial and central part of Christmas without which the thing becomes meaningless ...

Looking at different countries can give some ideas for a Christmas Eve meal, and Christmas Eve activities:

In **Poland**, the *Wigilia*, or Vigil meal starts when the youngest child in the family sees the first star in the evening sky. The table is laid with a white cloth, under which is placed some hay to recall the fact that Christ was born in a stable. The meal includes twelve different dishes – representing the twelve months of the year. In addition to fish, there is always a dish of *pierogi*, small Polish dumplings with various fillings. There is also borscht, and perhaps mushroom soup, herring, and various sweet things like poppy-seed cake. An important part of the meal is the sharing of the *oplatek*, or Christmas wafer: this is broken and passed around as a symbol of love and blessing. Sometimes pieces of wafer are posted with a Christmas message to family members who are far away. Midnight Mass is known as the *Pasterka*, or Shepherds' Mass, and begins – as do most Midnight Masses in Britain – with a time of carol singing as the church steadily fills with people.

In **Germany** and **Austria** the Christmas tree is decorated on the afternoon of Christmas Eve, with the smallest children being kept well out of the way until all is ready. As darkness falls, they are summoned – usually by the ringing of a little bell – to the Christmas room, where the tree is lit and glittering, there is Christmas music, and the presents are stacked enticingly. Some families keep up the tradition that it is the Christ-child himself who visits the house to leave gifts. Some say that the beautifully-decorated tree is the work of angels. It's still traditional to have real candles on the tree, though these are only lit for a short time and are carefully watched. Traditional German Christmas foods include Dresden *stollen*, which is a popular Christmas gift: a fruit bread with raisins, candied peel, almonds, raisins and currants. It is dredged with icing sugar and is delicious on its own or with butter.

In **Scandinavia** the evening meal includes various dishes, such as the Swedish *julskinka* ('Yule ham'), which is a tasty baked ham, and the **Norwegian** *lutefisk* or poached cod. There is also a tradition of eating a sort of creamy rice pudding – in some traditions this includes an almond, and whoever gets that has luck for the coming year. The gloriously-named *glogg* (mulled spiced wine with almonds and raisins) is a major feature of Christmas.

In **Finland**, Father Christmas is known as *Joulupukki*, which literally translates as 'Yule goat' or 'Christmas goat', and seems to date back to the days when people wore goatskin coats in winter. Today, he looks rather like the Americanized Santa Claus one sees everywhere, but he walks with a stick and he has a wife who makes unusually good Christmas rice pudding.

In **Sweden** the 'Christmas goat' is celebrated by goat ornaments and figures which are a central part of Christmas decorations.

In **Ireland**, families place a lighted candle in the window on Christmas Eve, to light the Holy Family on their journey to Bethlehem.

Christmas Day

Christmas morning traditionally means church bells ringing, presents stacked under the tree, hot spiced wine or other drinks, neighbourly chat, and excited children. It's nice to say Grace to start Christmas Dinner, even if we don't say it during the rest of the year:

> *Bless us, O Lord, and these, Thy gifts*
> *Which we are about to receive from Thy Bounty.*
> *Through Christ Our Lord, Amen.*

Roast turkey is still the most popular Christmas dish for the great meal, though some people opt for goose, and beef is making a big comeback. The Christmas Pudding, with its hidden silver charms or coins, is still an essential part of the meal. Most families have crackers, complete with terrible jokes and silly paper hats. It's traditional to toast 'absent friends'. Watching the Sovereign's annual Christmas broadcast used to be central to the day for many families – it's a worthwhile tradition that deserves to be fostered, and can include a loyal toast as the programme ends.

A large lunch can make for a sluggish afternoon – a lantern-lit walk can make a nice outing as darkness falls, and might even be combined with some carol singing!

Rather than just watch television all day, it's worth planning some (sedentary!) games and activities. Try the Christmas Quiz opposite (answers at the back of the book, and you will find some of them in the text too).

Some Traditional Games

Twenty Questions
Send someone out of the room and decide who he or she is to be – a figure from history, or someone prominent in public life, or a character from a book or film. When he returns he must work out who he is from just twenty questions, to which people may only answer 'yes' or 'no'. 'Am I alive?' 'Am I in a book?' 'Am I a child?' 'Am I female?' 'Was I in Parliament?' 'Did I fight a war?' 'Did I write books?' and so on.

A variant on this is for each person to be given a name on a label, stuck on his back. Everyone has to ask everyone else questions in order to establish identities. This is a good way of getting a mixed group of people talking. Every person is allowed to ask every other person just one question (or you could raise this to three questions if guest numbers are small) – and again the answer can only be 'yes' or 'no'.

Word-and-question
This comes from the children's classic *What Katy Did at School*. Everyone writes a word, preferably a noun, on a piece of paper, then passes the paper to the next person, who writes a question. Then all the pieces of paper are folded up, tossed into a box and mixed together. Each person draws one out and reads it. The idea is that you then write a poem which uses the word, and answers the question.

CHRISTMAS QUIZ

(Answers at the back of the book, or you may find some of them by reading through the text)

1. Which ruler of England made eating mince pies illegal?
2. What was the name of the angel who brought the news to Mary that she was to be the mother of the Saviour?
3. What are the traditional names of the Three Wise Men? In what European city are their remains said to be kept?
4. How is St Nicholas linked to pawnbrokers?
5. Who was St Wenceslas?
6. Which English King made the first-ever Christmas broadcast to Britain and the Empire?
7. What does the name 'Bethlehem' mean?
8. What do the letters 'AD' mean when written before a date, and how are they linked to Christmas?
9. How is the children's string game 'Cats Cradle' linked to Christmas?
10. To which country did Mary, Joseph, and the child Jesus flee to escape from Herod?
11. To which town did they return and make their home? What was Joseph's job?
12. What was the name of the husband of Mary's cousin Elizabeth?
13. When do we celebrate the birthday of John the Baptist?
14. When is Lady Day?
15. When is Candlemas and what does it commemorate?
16. What does *Gloria in excelsis deo* mean?
17. 'Behold a virgin shall conceive, and bear a son ...' Which prophet said these words in the Scriptures?
18. What does the word 'advent' mean?
19. When is Gaudete Sunday?
20. What does the word 'Epiphany' mean?
21. An account of Christ's birth is given in the Gospel of St Luke. Who was St Luke?
22. Who was Thomas Becket and why is he linked to Christmas?
23. Who was St Lucy and when is her feast-day?
24. What were the gifts brought to the infant Christ by the Wise Men and what do they signify?

Christmastide

There are lots of other days to celebrate in Christmastide: Christmas is not just for one day!

The Christmas season is technically forty days long – as is Easter. And the first twelve days are – as the old song reminds us – all Christmas Days. Many of them also have their own special significance.

We do not know whether or not the traditional song is actually a way of teaching Christian doctrine in a sort of code. In recent years it has become an established myth that this is so, and that Catholics used it for this purpose in the days of persecution – but no one really knows and there seems to be no consistent tradition of this, but rather a relatively modern invention of the story. However, the song can certainly work quite well as a means of memorizing aspects of the Faith, so it seems valuable to post it here.

The Twelve Days of Christmas

A partridge in a pear-tree (Christ, truly present in the Eucharist)
Two Turtle Doves (Old and New Testaments)
Three French hens (Three theological virtues: Faith, Hope, and Charity)
Four Calling Birds (Four Gospel writers: Matthew, Mark, Luke and John)
Five Gold Rings (Five books of the Old Testament: Genesis, Exodus, Leviticus, Numbers, Deuteronomy)
Six Geese a-laying (The six days of Creation)
Seven Swans a-swimming (Seven Sacraments: Baptism, Penance, Confirmation, Holy Communion, Anointing the Sick, Holy Orders, Matrimony)
Eights Maids a-milking (eight Beatitudes: Blessed are the poor in spirit; Blessed are those who mourn; Blessed are the meek; Blessed are those who hunger and thirst for righteousness; Blessed are the merciful; Blessed are the pure in heart; Blessed are those who are persecuted for righteousness)
Nine Ladies dancing (The nine fruits of the Holy Spirit: love, joy, peace, patience, kindliness, generosity, faithfulness, gentleness, self-control, as listed in Galatians 5:22)
Ten Lords a-leaping (The Ten Commandments)

Eleven Pipers piping (The eleven faithful Apostles, i.e. the original Twelve minus Judas)
Twelve Drummers drumming (The twelve points of doctrine in the Apostles' Creed).

Saints and Feast-days at Christmastide

St Stephen's Day: 26 December (Boxing Day)

Boxing Day doesn't refer to the sport of boxing. It refers to Christmas boxes – Christmas gifts. A 'Christmas Box' is the traditional name given to the small gift – today it's usually money but I remember when it could be a gift of cigarettes or beer – given to people who help us during the year: the dustmen, the postman, the paperboy. In recent times, alas, the giving of a 'Christmas box' has sometimes been linked to intimidation, so now some local authorities have formally banned the dustmen they employ from accepting (and certainly from demanding!) such gifts.

Boxing Day is a public holiday in Britain, which makes our Christmas something more relaxed and valuable than the American one-day event. It is traditionally a day for visiting family and friends, for a long country walk, for going to a pub, for eating the turkey cold with (my favourite dish!) bubble and squeak made from the leftover potatoes and Brussels sprouts (mashed together and fried).

If the weather is cold and dry, it's the perfect day for an outdoor picnic – turkey and ham sandwiches, slabs of Christmas cake, a walk to get rid of any sluggish feeling from the day before.

It is St Stephen's Day. He was the first Christian martyr, and is mentioned in the Acts of the Apostles: he is described as being 'full of grace and fortitude', and one who 'did great wonders and signs among the people'. There is a wonderful account of his preaching, explaining how God had prepared for the coming of his Son and how all things were to be fulfilled in Christ. This angered his opponents:

> And they crying out with a loud voice, stopped their ears and with one accord ran violently upon him. And casting him out from the city, they stoned him; and the witnesses laid down their garments at the feet of a young man whose name was Saul. And they stoned Stephen, who invoked saying 'Lord Jesus, receive my spirit'. And

falling on his knees, he cried with a loud voice, saying: 'Lord, lay not this sin to their charge'. And when he had said this, he fell asleep in the Lord. And Saul was consenting to his death.

(Acts 7:57–59)

In Ireland, St Stephen's Day was traditionally the day for going from house to house begging for pennies, carrying a decorated bush on a pole with a pretend bird in it, a wren – pronounced 'ran'. No one seems to know the origins of this, although there are various legends concerning Christ and a wren. The traditional rhyme to be chanted is:

> The wren, the wren, the king of all birds
> St Stephen's day was caught in the furze
> Up with the penny and down with the pan
> Give us a penny to bury the wren

Because of a nineteenth-century Christmas carol, St Stephen's Day is also linked, in the minds of many English-speaking people, to St Wenceslas. He was a king of Bohemia (in the modern-day Czech republic) who was a devout Christian, and was murdered by his pagan brother Boleslas. His only link with Christmas is that the carol – which does not originate in Bohemia at all – described him as looking out of his window into the snowy fields 'on the feast of Stephen', and helping a poor beggar there in a Christian spirit.

Mulled Ale for St Stephen's Day

Peel and core half a dozen apples and bake them in the oven until they are soft. Then slice them into a bowl. Heat up two pints of ale or cider, add two tablespoons of brown sugar, and a quarter of a teaspoon each of grated nutmeg, cinnamon, and ginger. Bring to the boil, but do not let it boil for very long, just time enough for the sugar to dissolve. Then pour this mixture over the sliced apples in a bowl. Leave to stand for the space of one *Pater Noster*. Then serve it, in mugs or thick glasses around which you have wrapped napkins.

This is sometimes known as 'Lambs' Wool' because of the soft fluffy look of the baked apples.

This mulled ale is also excellent for Wassailing on New Year's Eve!

St John's Day: 28 December

St John was the 'Apostle whom Jesus loved' and the one who took care of Mary following Jesus' Crucifixion. Tradition says that, alone of all the Apostles, he did not himself suffer a martyr's death and lived to a serene old age, preaching and teaching the love of God, a witness radiant in his faith. His preaching brought him exile to the island of Patmos, and he finally died at Ephesus. St Jerome says of him that in old age when asked to preach he would simply tell people 'Love one another. That is the Lord's command.' He wrote the Gospel which bears his name, with its magnificent opening words: 'In the beginning was the Word . . .' which we hear read aloud at many Christmas carol services.

John was a fisherman from Galilee, the brother of James. He was present with Peter on the first Easter morning, running to the tomb and then standing back to let Peter enter first. It was he who first recognized the risen Christ by the Sea of Tiberias. He was later imprisoned, along with Peter, and also went with him to preach in Samaria.

Sometimes the days immediately following Christmas Day can be quiet and dull for residents in old people's homes – St John's Day would be a good day for a visit, with a group to sing carols and pass round some mince pies.

There is also a very attractive tradition of mulled wine on St John's Day. It should be drunk as a loving cup (each person taking a sip and then passing it on) – a nice thing to do at supper on this night. (See the recipe for 'Bishop's wine' for St Nicholas, 6 December).

According to Christian legend, John travelled around Judea with Peter, and then went on to Asia Minor, where he founded the Seven Churches referred to in Revelation. Legend also has it that the Emperor Domitian twice attempted to kill him: once by ordering him to drink a cup of poisoned wine. St John took and blessed the cup – and the poison slithered away in the form of a snake. Because of this legend, there is in many countries a tradition on the day of his feast: a blessing of wine, in his name. Often a special wine is prepared. At the dinner on that day, the father blesses the cup, then each member of the family takes a drink, saying to the others 'I drink to you in the love of St John'. Even children get a little sip.

John is said to have died at Ephesus as a very old man, having

35

written his great Gospel, three Epistles, and the Book of Revelation.

Evelyn Birge Witz
A Continual Feast: A Cookbook to celebrate the joys of family and faith throughout the Christian year

Holy Innocents' Day: 28 December

A voice in Rama was heard, lamentation and great mourning; Rachel bewailing her children, and would not be comforted, because they are not. (Jer. 31)

This day honours the Holy Innocents – the boy-children in Bethlehem who were slaughtered on the orders of King Herod because he was looking for the Christ-child. Their death has always been seen as foreshadowing that of Christ's on the Cross. They are also symbolic of all innocent and suffering children. In the twentieth century there were many slaughtered children – those in the Ukraine in the 1930s who starved to death in the famine in the days of Stalin, those in Poland and elsewhere in the Second World War who were killed in concentration camps, those in China who died in the 1960s famine under Mao. To these we could perhaps add the babies killed through abortion since it has become widespread in our own country and elsewhere since the 1960s, and those who die because of poverty and hunger in Africa and Asia. And there are children who suffer, and whose innocence is destroyed: teenage and pre-teenage girls used in brothels in Asia and in Europe, children orphaned by war or by disease, especially in Africa (Aids), children enduring the misery of parental break-up or divorce, children used in the making of pornography or caught up in crime or drug-addiction, children denied proper moral formation and family life.

28 December has by tradition been a day for honouring children – but with a serious side. It used to be known as 'Saint Cross Day', looking ahead to the Crucifixion. It was considered a bad day on which to start any new venture because – like the lives of the Holy Innocents – it would not reach fulfilment. It was thus an unpopular day for weddings (unlike St Stephen's Day, which was popular, as families were in any case gathering together for the Christmas celebrations, so it was useful to combine events).

At that hour the disciples came to Jesus, saying: Who thinkest thou art the greater in the kingdom of Heaven?

And Jesus, calling unto him a little child, set him in the midst of them, and said: 'Amen I say to you, unless you be converted, and become as little children, you shall not enter into the kingdom of Heaven. Whosoever therefore shall humble himself as this little child, he is the greater in the kingdom of Heaven. And he that shall receive one such little child in my name, receives me. But he that shall scandalize one of these little ones that believe in me, it were better for him that a millstone should be hanged around his neck, and that he should be drowned in the depths of the sea.'

(Matthew 18:1–6)

In some abbeys and monasteries, 28 December is a day when the youngest and newest novice is treated as the abbot for the day, and/or must choose some celebrations and festivities to mark the day. He is named 'Innocent' and presides at a festive meal in the evening.

There was a long tradition of throwing a party for choirboys and for altar servers on Holy Innocents' Day, to thank them for their work in church over the Christmas Masses and to launch them on a few days' well-deserved holiday until Epiphany.

Apparently there was also an old tradition that children should be spanked on this day to remind them of the sufferings of the Innocents!

St Thomas Becket: 29 December

This is a Christmas saint – he was martyred during this Christmas season, which added greatly to the legend that grew up around him. He remains a controversial figure, although for centuries venerated as a saint.

Born in London in the early twelfth century to a well-to-do Norman family, Thomas Becket was educated by the monks at Merton Abbey on the banks of the river Wandle, not far from Wimbledon (the ruins can be seen today, under a shopping centre!). He later studied at Paris, Bologna and Auxerre, and then obtained a post in the household of the Archbishop of Canterbury, Theobald, who gave him several important tasks including some diplomatic missions to Rome. He became, in due course, archdeacon of Canterbury and later Lord Chancellor. He was extremely loyal to the King, Henry II, and they became personal friends, Henry sending his young son to be educated in Thomas' household.

Archbishop Theobald died in April 1161, and in May Thomas

was appointed in his stead. It was not a popular choice – as Chancellor he had enforced the king's rules with regard to collecting church taxes and it was assumed he would always put the king's interests first.

Thomas himself thought differently – from the start he warned the king that he would have to put the Church first, and that he could not 'serve two masters'.

These were complicated days in the Church. Thomas was a warm supporter of the Pope, Alexander III. He was also a strong defender of the Church's rights, and began to make it clear that he would not allow the King to interfere in any way with church property or church matters.

Tensions with the King erupted into open argument. In 1164 Thomas, fearing for his life, fled to France. He sought the support of the Pope but only partially secured it. Henry by now was enraged, and what had begun as a dispute over property and taxes was by now out of control. In December 1170 Thomas returned to England, landing at Sandwich in Kent.

King Henry, infuriated, is said to have shouted 'Who will rid me of this turbulent priest?' and four knights took this as a call to arms and hurried to Canterbury. Thomas was at Vespers in the Cathedral. The knights rushed in and attacked him savagely, striking him in the head and leaving a trail of blood across the floor of the Cathedral as his body slumped before the altar.

As news of the martyrdom spread, stories of Thomas' sanctity spread too: his personal penances, his devotion to prayer. His tomb in the Cathedral became a place of pilgrimage. In 1174 Henry knelt in penance before it. Canterbury had a Christmas martyr and England had a legend. From Geoffrey Chaucer's *Canterbury Tales* to T. S. Eliot's *Murder in the Cathedral*, Thomas of Canterbury has inspired prose and poetry, pilgrims and stories, speeches and drama. Centuries later, another Henry and another Thomas – Henry VII and Thomas More, would be involved in another drama and another martyrdom. The names are woven into the tapestry of English history.

Collecting alms for the poor in December – going from house to house – was known in medieval times as 'Thomassing', and was a central part of Christmas care for the poor for centuries. It was probably associated with 21 December, which was then marked as the feast-day of St Thomas the Apostle, but seems to have been linked with St Thomas Becket too.

Telling the story of Thomas Becket, perhaps with some reading from Eliot's play, or acting it out with lots of dressing-up (bishop's robes, knights in armour with swords, monks chanting) could work well on a winter's afternoon and could finish with hot drinks and Christmas food.

St Sylvester: 31 December
(Hogmanay; New Year's Eve)

The year ends with Hogmanay, New Year's Eve, the feast of St Sylvester. He was an early pope, and he died in Rome in 335. By tradition, his feast-day, coming as it does on the last day of the year, is celebrated with fireworks at midnight – a tradition in mainland Europe which has now come to Britain where it has merged with other New Year's Eve festivities. We sing 'Auld lang syne', drink champagne, listen to the chimes of Big Ben on the television or radio, pull crackers, wear paper hats.

'Auld lang syne' is one of those songs that people think they know, but often don't. It is traditionally sung on the stroke of midnight and goes like this:

> Should auld acquaintance be forgot
> And never brought to mind?
> Should auld acquaintance be forgot
> For the sake of auld lang syne?
> *For auld lang syne, my friends*
> *For auld lang syne*
> *We'll tak' a cup o' kindness yet*
> *For the sake of auld lang syne.*

Then comes the important bit: cross your arms and take the hands of the people on either side of you, as you sing:

> So gie's a hand my trusty friend
> And here's a hand o' mine
> We'll tak' a cup o' kindness yet
> For the sake of auld lang syne
> *For auld lang syne, my friends*
> *For auld lang syne*
> *We'll tak' a cup o' kindness yet*
> *For the sake of auld lang syne.*

Note that you're not meant to take hands until the second verse. The first verse is simply sung with everyone standing in a circle. (On New Year's Eve 1999, at the big televised celebrations to mark the start of the year 2000, the Queen was the only one who got it right.)

First Footing

By tradition, the first person into the house for the New Year should be dark-haired, and carrying some fuel (a piece of coal or wood) and something to drink (glass of whisky). This is meant to ensure that the household does not lack fuel or food in the year ahead.

In our family, we have a tradition of singing old songs round the piano on New Year's Eve. If you don't know the words, a trawl on the Internet will actually find most of them. Plan beforehand and get the words written out so that everyone has a copy, to avoid that 'Oh, um, how does it go?' syndrome where no one knows anything except the first line! Try 'On Ilkley Moor Bar T'at', 'Pack up your troubles in your old kit-bag', 'It's a long way to Tipperary', and songs from twentieth-century musicals 'Oh what a beautiful mornin'', 'Supercalifragilisticexpealidocious!', 'A Spoonful of Sugar'.

A particularly satisfying thing to do is to divide the group into two: one half sings 'Pack up your troubles' and the other 'It's a long way to Tipperary'. The tunes partly mesh together and partly contradict. Most satisfying.

A Yorkshire guest at one of the New Year parties told us that the original version of the popular carol 'While shepherds watched their flocks by night' was sung to the tune of 'On Ilkley Moor Bar T'at'. Try it: it works extremely well!

Some hymns are excellent for this sort of community singing round a piano at home: try 'Praise my soul, the king of Heaven' or 'Who would true valour see?' You could finish with 'The day thou gavest, Lord, is ended' or perhaps the '*Salve Regina*'.

Wassailing

An old tradition was to go 'wassailing' – visiting from house to house, sharing a mug of ale and wishing a blessing on the house and everyone in it for the New Year. Wassailers carried a decorated branch – some Christmas greenery tied to a tall pole, with red ribbons and Christmas-tree style decorations on it.

> *God bless the master of this house*
> *God bless the mistress too*
> *And all the little children*
> *That round the table go.*

> *Love and joy come to you*
> *And to you your Wassail too*
> *And God bless you and grant you a Happy New Year*
> *And God grant you a happy New Year!*
> *Anon*

Epiphany

> We three kings of Orient are
> Bearing gifts, we traverse afar
> Field and fountain, moor and mountain
> Following yonder star.

> *O, star of wonder, star of light*
> *Star of royal beauty bright*
> *Westward leading, still proceeding*
> *Guide us to thy perfect Light.*
> *Traditional carol*

The word 'epiphany' means 'manifestation', or 'showing'. It marks the showing of the infant Christ to the wider world, and specifically to the Three Magi, who came from the East to worship him. The Feast of the Epiphany is 6 January, twelve days after Christmas – hence the tradition of the Twelve Days of Christmas. At present – and I think this is rather a pity – the Catholic Bishops of England and Wales have announced that the Epiphany should be marked on the Sunday nearest to 6 January, instead of having a day on its own. Anyway, it certainly deserves a celebration.

In parts of southern Europe, and in Latin America, Epiphany is the day on which children receive their Christmas presents. In Italy, the day is known as *Befana* – a corruption of the word 'Epiphany' – and the gifts come via a witch of that name. One tradition is to have a sort of cauldron, or big box or other container, in which lots

41

of small gifts are hidden in sawdust or shredded paper. Children dive their hands into the cauldron to find their gifts, and some of the little parcels turn out to be blanks, while others contain sweets, small gifts and toys.

The traditional dish for Epiphany is a *Galette des Rois*. I first sampled this with French friends while we were all living in Berlin. The galette is simple to make – essentially it is two layers of puff pastry with a layer of marzipan between. Somewhere in the marzipan the cook places a small figure of a king or – if you don't have one of those – a dried bean. Whoever gets the dried bean/king becomes King or Queen for the evening. Two lovely golden crowns should be on the table, and the king wears one and chooses someone to be the queen. They can then be addressed as 'Your Majesty'. If this is a children's party, everyone might line up to bow or curtsy, and the King or Queen might be given the task of distributing small packets of sweets in a regal fashion to all present, or announcing the next game.

Galette des Rois

> 1 packet of frozen puff-pastry (or make your own according to your favourite recipe)
> Marzipan
> Circular flan dish

Roll out the pastry so that it is large enough to accommodate two circles that can be fitted into the flan dish, one on top of the other. Roll out the marzipan and cut out one circle. Grease the flan dish lightly with butter, place the first pastry circle inside, then the marzipan (with a dried bean somewhere in it, not right in the centre). Top with the other pastry circle. Use the odds and ends of pastry to make a leaf design, or a cross, or an 'E' for Epiphany, or whatever you like, on top. Bake in a moderately hot oven for approximately 7–10 minutes. Serve with whipped cream, and with cups of freshly-brewed coffee.

The *Galette* works well as part of supper, or as an 'elevenses' treat – perhaps at a coffee-morning organized by some church group?

It is traditional to leave two slices at the end of the meal to give away, in the name of Christ and his mother – perhaps an elderly neighbour would like a slice, with a friendly visit?

Star Singers

In Austria and Germany, the Star Singers visit houses on or around Epiphany. Three children, representing the Three Magi, carrying boxes representing the gifts of gold, frankincense, and myrrh as described in the Scriptures, go from house to house, singing carols and receiving money which goes to charity. They are led by someone carrying a star on a tall pole. I remember some delightful Star Singers in Oetz: the one designated for frankincense carrying the incense-burner from church, and swinging it as he walked through the snow, giving a lovely scented trail. I followed and, to my delight, discovered it led to the house where I was staying, where the boys recited poems and were generously rewarded.

The Star Singers bring a blessing with them: the house is blessed for the New Year, and the initials of the three Kings: 'K+M+B', for Kaspar, Melchior, and Balthasar, are chalked up over the front door.

It would be delightful to start a Star Singers tradition in Britain.

A Piñata

The word means 'pineapple', because that's what it looks like. It's a tradition from South America. Blow up a balloon, then mix up some wallpaper paste and tear newspapers into small pieces. Cover the whole balloon with two or three thicknesses of newspaper pieces. Leave it in a warm place to dry for about twelve hours. Then stick in a pin and pop the balloon. Cut off the top of the piñata carefully (you will be replacing it shortly). Paint the piñata red or green to look Christmassy, and cover it with Christmas stickers, stars, long Christmas streamers, etc. The lid should be decorated too. Now fill the inside with sweets, nuts, and small toys. Replace the top (you may need to stick it on with sticky tape). Now hang up the piñata (string attached with firm sticky tape) At some point in the celebrations, invite children to bash it with their shoes. It will break, and the toys and sweets will shower down for everyone to enjoy.

Twelfth Night

Epiphany is the last of the Twelve Days of Christmas, so it's right to have a celebration. In Britain, this is by long tradition the day on which we dismantle the Christmas tree and take down other decorations. The *Galette* can be a special treat at supper, but there could also be some crackers, candles, mince pies and perhaps some singing of carols, especially those which tell of the Three Kings. Then the last nice chocolate things from the tree are distributed and enjoyed, and the decorations are tissue-wrapped and put away in boxes until next year.

Although today we take down decorations on Twelfth Night, an older tradition says they should be kept up until Candlemas – February 2nd! It might be fun to leave up just one token decoration – a sprig of holly behind a picture, or behind the kitchen clock? It can then be taken down at Candlemas, with one more final taste of Christmas fare.

Plough Sunday/Plough Monday

In former times, the first Monday after 6 January was Plough Monday, the day when work started again after the Christmas celebrations, so the day before was Plough Sunday, when a plough would be brought into church to be blessed. Plough Monday itself was celebrated with a final special meal, eating up the remains of the Christmas food.

St Agnes: 21 January

> St Agnes Eve – ah bitter chill it was!
> The owl, for all his feathers, was a-cold
> The hare limp'd trembling through the frozen grass
> And silent was the flock in woolly fold.
> John Keats 1795–1821

St Agnes was a young Roman martyr – we hear her name mentioned in the Canon of the Mass, along with other young heroines of those early days of the Church, such as Cecilia, Agatha, and Lucy. She showed courage and faith, and a determination to hold

44

on to her Christian beliefs and Christian morals.

The name Agnes means 'lamb'. A Metropolitan archbishop wears a pallium, a woollen stole, around his neck and shoulders, which is given to him by the Pope at a ceremony in Rome, to emphasize the unity of the Church. Each pallium is made of wool from lambs presented to the Pope on St Agnes Day in Rome.

One tradition says that on the eve of St Agnes – i.e. on the evening of 20 January – a young girl who wants to know about her future husband should comb her hair by candlelight near an open window, looking into a mirror. She will see a ghostly image of her future husband in the shadows over her right shoulder!

But the story of St Agnes is really about courage, and early writers about her, notably St Ambrose, emphasized this.

> It is the blessed Virgin Agnes' feast, for today she was sanctified by shedding her innocent blood, and gave to Heaven her Heaven-claimed spirit.
> She that was too young to be a bride was old enough to be a martyr and that too in an age when men were faltering in faith, and even hoary heads grew wearied and denied our God.
>
> Attrib. St Ambrose, 4th century

Conversion of St Paul: 25 January

If you read the Acts of the Apostles, you will find a very gripping account of the martyrdom of St Stephen – whose feast we marked, of course, on the first day after Christmas Day – describing how he was stoned to death. There is an interesting detail. The men stoning him left their cloaks at the feet of a man named Saul.

Saul was a great persecutor of Christians. He saw them as undermining the ancient faith that had been passed down by God. But something happened to him. On the road to Damascus – where he was heading to carry out further assaults on the small Christian community – he was struck by a great light and left blinded. As he lay on the ground he heard a voice from Heaven which called out 'Saul, Saul, why do you persecute me?' It was the voice of Christ. Led to the Christians, he received the fullness of the Faith and went on to become one of the greatest Christian teachers of all time, and a martyr for Christ.

The feast of the Conversion of St Paul marks all of this, and is significantly exactly one month after Christmas – a privileged date which gives St Paul due status. We still have his letters read out to us at Mass, and his message is still central to our lives because it is the message of Christ. We know quite a lot about St Paul's adventures – how he was shipwrecked (tradition says on Malta, where he is still much venerated), how he went to Ephesus and won people over from the cult of Diana, how he was flogged and imprisoned. The significance of St Paul's life cannot be underestimated.

Historically, this was a most important feast-day in Britain. It was chosen for Royal weddings, for example that of James IV of Scotland to Princess Margaret of England in 1503. And in old St Paul's, in the Middle Ages, there was a great festival at St Paul's Cathedral in London in which deer were brought right into the cathedral to be given to the dean and chapter as a celebration gift. The servant in charge of all the arrangements was rewarded with five shillings (25p in today's money – but worth a great deal more at that time) and a loaf of bread stamped with an image of St Paul's.

It's also a day for watching the weather. Check it with this old rhyme:

> If St Paul's day be fair and clear
> It does betide a happy year;
> But if by chance it snow or rain,
> Then will be dear [expensive] all kinds of grain;
> If clouds or mist do dark the skie
> Great store of birds and beasts shall die;
> And if the winds do fly aloft
> Then war shall vex the kingdome oft.

Candlemas: 2 February

Candlemas falls on 2 February, and marks the end of the Christmas season. It is the old English name for the feast of the Presentation in the Temple – marking the day when, as the Scriptures tell us, Mary and Joseph fulfilled the Jewish law and custom by taking their little baby boy to the Temple to present him to God. They took along birds to sacrifice, two young doves. It was an important ritual for the first-born. But something special happened. Simeon, an old man who spent his days in the Temple in prayer, took the child in his arms and made a great prophesy about him: 'This child will be a light to lighten the gentiles, and the glory of his people, Israel.' Simeon had been waiting for the Messiah, and trusting in God. In

46

words that have been sung and prayed in churches around the world many thousands of times since, he praised God and said 'Now, Lord, you let your servant depart in peace, according to your promise – because my eyes have seen your salvation, the salvation you promised to your people, Israel.'

In commemoration of this event – the infant Christ being proclaimed as the salvation of the world – we light candles at Mass. It is very beautiful to go to an evening Mass on the Feast of the Presentation, and to hold a lighted candle during the solemn reading of the Gospel, hearing Simeon's words and seeing the glowing lights, and people's faces. The light of Christ has indeed spread to us, the gentiles, and is the light of all nations now and into the future.

We can take our candles home with us and light them again at the supper table. One reason why Candlemas became a popular feast was that, with spring approaching and the evenings getting longer, people were happy to use up old candle-ends in celebration, knowing that they would not be needed as winter's long dark evenings receded.

An old saying was 'Candlemas, candle-less'. And in Germany, the saying used to be 'Mary blows the light out, Michael lights it again' (*Maria blasts Licht aus, Michel zunds wieder am*) – because on St Michael's Day, Michaelmas, in September, it is time to light up the candles again as the evenings are getting long and dark. In America, 2 February is known as 'Groundhog Day': presumably because these animals come out of hibernation at this time.

Candlemas used to be the day on which Christmas decorations were taken down. If you have decided to keep up a link with this old custom, and kept just one sprig of holly or mistletoe up somewhere in the house, tonight it can be taken down and tossed out – with perhaps something Christmassy at supper to mark the occasion. Save a jar of mincemeat for Candlemas and enjoy some mince pies!

St Blaise: 3 February

The feast of St Blaise falls immediately after Candlemas, on 3 February, and is linked to it as the celebrations also involve candles.

Blaise was a bishop, and a martyr. It is said that, as he was being led to his martyrdom, a mother in the crowd pushed her way forward and begged him to bless and heal her child, who was choking on a fish-bone. The good Bishop took the little boy and placed his hands on his throat – the child coughed up the fish-bone and was instantly well.

Because of his miracle, the aid of St Blaise is invoked for sore throats and coughs. On his feast-day, many churches have a traditional Blessing of Throats. Two candles are crossed and held over the throat of each person, who comes to kneel in front of the priest at the altar rail, and a special blessing is said.

If there is no St Blaise blessing in your church, why not ask if this lovely custom could be revived?

St Valentine: 14 February

I was almost reluctant to include St Valentine's Day in this book, as it has become so extraordinarily vulgar and silly in recent years, and has lost most of its charm. In any case, you will not find St Valentine on this date in any church calendar now – it is instead the feast of Saints Cyril and Methodius, the great Apostles of the Slavs, joint patrons with St Benedict of the continent of Europe.

There is a church dedicated to St Valentine in Rome but not much is known about him. The tradition that 14 February is his feast-day is certainly an old one – Shakespeare mentions it in *A Midsummer Night's Dream*. It was said to be the day on which birds chose their mates and made their nests. For a long while, the day was hall-marked by a sense of innocence – a Valentine card, usually very charmingly decorated with hearts and flowers and pieces of ribbon and lace – could be sent anonymously to indicate affection, perhaps with some coded message that would indicate the sender. It was a day for declaring love, a good day on which to propose marriage. In the late nineteenth and early twentieth centuries, the idea of home-made Valentine cards caught on, and children would make them for their parents, little girls for their best friends.

Today – well, every restaurant seems to be offering special dinners, and tables get booked up weeks in advance. There are horrible Valentine cards with contraceptives attached, and crude ones with unfunny messages.

Can we salvage something of the true meaning of St Valentine's Day? There are still some pretty cards to be found. A cake baked

48

in the shape of a heart might be a nice treat at supper. A posy of flowers is always, always, an acceptable gift from a fiancé or husband. And, as it happens, I do know of some very delightful couples who became engaged on St Valentine's Day and it made a happy and romantic start to marriage.

Lent – Forty Days

The date of Easter – the great Christian feast marking our redemption – is connected to the Jewish Passover, and falls in the spring. Easter Sunday is always on the Sunday of the first full moon after the spring equinox (i.e. the day when we have equal hours of light and darkness).

Lent is the period – always forty days long – of renewal, penance and prayer that leads up to the great drama of Holy Week and Easter. It always falls in springtime – the season when the earth itself is in a process of renewal and new life.

In the Old Testament, Moses led the people of Israel for forty years in the desert. In the New, Christ spent forty days fasting and praying in the desert at the start of his public ministry. Seasons in the Church are always forty days long – Christmas is forty days from Christmas Eve to Candlemas. Lent is forty days from Ash Wednesday until Holy Saturday. Easter is forty days from Easter Sunday until the feast of the Ascension.

Lent is a season of penance. Within living memory, it was quite strictly observed in traditional Catholic parts of Europe. Long ago, the Lenten fast was kept by everyone except children, the sick, and the very old: no meat, and no eggs or dairy products. This is partly why the tradition of Easter eggs arose – because any eggs laid by the hens during Lent were kept and preserved and used for the celebrations at Easter. Hence also the great traditions of Easter foods – cheesecake, and simnel cake, and roast lamb.

Today, the Church reminds us that Lent is still important, still a season of penance. Each of us should observe it by renouncing something for this season – chocolate, alcohol, sweet things, snacks between meals. Many families have a simple Lenten meal on Fridays, and give the money thus saved to charity. The no-meat tradition also still lingers, and fish dishes and vegetable dishes are appropriate for Lent.

Because of this, Lent begins with a day on which we eat up the last of the rich food and enjoy a party – hence Pancake Day.

Shrove Tuesday – Carnival and Pancakes

The name 'Shrove Tuesday' comes from the old English word for going to confession – we are 'scraped' or 'shriven' of our sins. It is the same word that gives us the word 'scribe' and 'inscription', and the German *schreib*, meaning write. When we are released from our sins, it is as though we are being scraped clean!

Shrovetide is therefore a reminder of a central part of Lent – confessing our sins and receiving absolution for them.

The name 'Mardi Gras' means 'Fat Tuesday', and the tradition of pre-Lent feasting is deeply embedded in Catholic tradition.

The tradition of pancakes comes from the idea of eating up the eggs and cream and milk before Lent begins. The pancakes are traditionally eaten with brown sugar and a squeeze of lemon juice, but there are lots of other tasty fillings that are good to try, too.

Pancakes

> 6 oz flour
> 1 egg
> Milk

Place the flour in a bowl and break the egg into it, then slowly stir and beat until it becomes sticky, adding the milk gradually until it becomes the thickness of golden syrup. You can simply double the amounts of flour, eggs, and milk according to how many people are coming to your pancake party! Be warned – people will eat a lot of pancakes.

Put a small amount of oil in the frying pan and heat it up. Pour in a spoonful or two of batter and swirl it round so that it covers the bottom of the pan. When it is cooked, flip it over and cook it on the other side.

Traditionally, each pancake should be tossed three times – in honour of the Trinity! If you can't manage that, everyone should at least have a try at tossing a pancake just once.

Some towns and villages have pancake races, in which people compete, running with a frying pan and a (usually artificial) pancake which has to be tossed three times en route.

A pancake can be served rolled up, with various accompaniments:

Small snips of bacon fried up with chopped onion
Sliced fried mushrooms
Fried tomatoes

Lemon juice and honey
Lemon juice and brown sugar or golden syrup
Strawberry jam, melted, with or without whipped cream
Chocolate sauce and/or ice cream

'Goodbye to meat!' That is the origin of the word 'carnival' which comes from the Latin word for meat (which also gives us words like 'carnivorous', meaning a meat-eating animal) and *vale*, which means 'farewell' or 'goodbye'. The original carnival tradition was that of a pre-Lent celebration. The early spring is still traditionally Carnival time in some parts of Europe, and in South America. This was also a time for pre-Lent weddings, notably in Ireland: because the Church used to discourage celebration of marriage during the penitential season of Lent, people somehow thought that the right time to marry was immediately before Lent began!

In Britain, the old name for the day before Shrove Tuesday was 'Collop Monday', collops being the final scraps of bacon eaten up before Lent (so snips of bacon with your pancakes is definitely traditional).

The traditional idea of Carnival is that it is a time of fun which ends with solemnity – think of the old-style clown doll, always painted with a tear on his cheek. Think of the song 'The Carnival is over'. Carnival ends with a sudden recognition that, at midnight on Shrove Tuesday, Lent begins.

Ash Wednesday

'Remember, man, that thou art dust, and to dust thou shalt return.'
'Repent, and believe in the Gospel.'

Ashes are an ancient symbol of sorrow and repentance. We speak of someone 'wearing sackcloth and ashes' when they need to express public repentance.

On Ash Wednesday, ashes will be distributed at church. Each person will receive ashes on his forehead, in the form of a cross.The ashes are made by burning palms from last year's Palm Sunday. The blessing of ashes at the start of the Ash Wednesday Mass makes a dramatic start to Lent.

As Lent begins, we embark on a time of penance and prayer: each one of us will think of something specific that we will do: giving up chocolate, or alcohol, or between-meals snacks. One possibility is to give up watching television during Lent (it can be done!).

Most Catholic parishes, groups, and schools have a charity to which they donate during Lent. The idea is that the money given comes from genuine sacrifices made – money that has not been spent on sweets, magazines, snacks, cups of coffee, and small treats.

What about some special venture for Lent? Why don't we all do something worthwhile like

- put on rubber gloves (or plastic bags over our hands) and collect all the litter in the street? Put the glass and plastic bottles in the recycling bins and seal up the rest in bin-bags and put it out for collection with our own domestic rubbish.
- clean up some local graffiti? A lot can be achieved with a bottle of white spirit and a scrubbing-brush. Make it a team effort with some friends?
- organize some music and gifts for Easter at a local old people's home? They may get carol singers at Christmas, but do they get anything at Easter? Are there some singers who might create a small group and sing some songs/madrigals/hymns?
- get to daily Mass?
- spend time in adoration of the Blessed Sacrament each week?

In some countries, every Friday in Lent is a day of abstinence from meat. In Britain, this is not the case, but Ash Wednesday and Good Friday are both days of fasting (one main meal and a couple of light snacks) and abstinence (no meat). Under church law, this binds everyone over the age of fourteen and under sixty-five, except of course the sick.

I am indebted to the Sisters at the Benedictine convent at Minster in Thanet (Kent) for this Vegetarian Loaf, which might be a suitable Lenten dish:

6 oz red lentils
8 fl. oz water

4 oz grated cheese
1 onion, chopped
2 oz mushrooms, chopped
1^1/$_2$ oz breadcrumbs
1 tablespoon chopped parsley
^{1}/$_4$ teaspoon salt
Freshly ground pepper
1 teaspoon lemon juice
^{1}/$_4$ teaspoon powdered garlic
1 egg

Place the lentils and water into a saucepan and simmer gently until the lentils are tender and most of the water absorbed. Drain well. Set the oven to gas mark 5, 375°F. Grease a 1lb loaf tin and put a strip of non-stick paper on the bottom. Add the grated cheese, onion, mushrooms, breadcrumbs, chopped parsley, lemon juice and egg to the lentils, mixing well. Season with plenty of salt and pepper. Spoon the mixture into the tin and bake uncovered for about 45 minutes.

The Sisters add 'This loaf is good either hot or cold and slices well. If served hot, it is good with a mushroom sauce, and if cold with some home-made chutney!'

They also have this Lentil Soup – which is even more suitable for Lent as it doesn't include any eggs:

1 large onion, peeled and chopped
1 tablespoon olive oil
8 oz split red lentils
1 litre stock or water
1–2 tablespoons lemon juice
^{1}/$_4$ teaspoon salt
Freshly ground black pepper
^{1}/$_4$ teaspoon dried herbs

Heat the oil in a fairly large saucepan and fry the onion for about 5 minutes, until it's lightly browned. Add the lentils and water and bring up to the boil, then leave the soup to simmer gently for about 20 minutes until the lentils are soft. Add lemon juice and season with salt and black pepper and herbs. Reheat before serving.

This vegetarian soup is nutritious and our hungry guests arriving on a Friday night love the delicious smell as it simmers in our Guest House kitchen.

From a Benedictine Kitchen – Recipes from Minster Abbey.

A LENTEN QUIZ

(You'll know many of the answers if you've been reading this book carefully!)

1. What is the origin of the word 'carnival'?
2. What does 'Mardi Gras' mean?
3. Of what are the ashes made that are used in church on Ash Wednesday?
4. On what day of the week did the Last Supper take place?
5. How many thieves were crucified with Jesus on Calvary?
6. What does 'shriving' mean?
7. Holy Thursday is sometimes called Maundy Thursday. What does 'Maundy' actually mean?
8. What is the Royal Maundy?
9. How long is Lent?
10. For how many days did Christ fast and pray in the desert?
11. For how many years did Moses lead the Israelites through the desert?
12. Which Apostle betrayed Jesus?
13. Which Apostle denied Jesus three times but repented and wept bitterly about it?

Some Saints' Days in Lent

It is traditional to let up on any Lenten fasting if there is a genuine feast-day. There are several saints' days that may fall in Lent:

St David: 1 March

Patron saint of Wales, the name is Dewi in Welsh. Son of a Cardigan chieftain and St Non or Nonna. He founded a line of twelve monasteries across Wales, and became a bishop. His main monastery was at the place now named after him in Pembrokeshire. His symbols are a daffodil and a leek: it is traditional to wear a daffodil on St David's Day.

There are lots of good recipes involving leeks: a leek pie, leek-and-potato soup, or simply leeks served in a white sauce with a mixture of grated cheese and breadcrumbs on top, heated under the grill so that the cheese melts.

Leek pie

Shortcrust pastry to line a flan dish

Mixture:

> 3 leeks, washed and sliced
> 1 egg
> $1/2$ pint of creamy milk
> A little salt
> $1/2$ teaspoon mixed herbs

In a frying pan, slightly cook the leeks in a little butter or oil. Mix together the beaten egg, milk, herbs, and salt, add the leeks and pour this mixture into the flan case. Bake for 30 minutes on a moderate heat until the mixture has set.

St Patrick: 17 March

Born in what is now Wales, the son of a Romano-British chieftain, taken to Ireland by pirates, he worked in slavery before winning his freedom and eventually going home. He trained to be a priest in Gaul (France) and finally became a missionary bishop in Ireland. He used the shamrock to teach about the Trinity – it still blooms only in Ireland and is of course the national symbol – and called down heavenly fire to show the Druids the power of the one true God.

The traditional dish to eat on St Patrick's Day is boiled bacon and cabbage. You buy a good piece of boiling bacon or ham – say $1^1/2$ pounds – and boil it allowing 25 minutes per pound and then a further 15 minutes. Then use the same water to boil up the cabbage, which you cook very quickly so that it is not too soggy. Slice the bacon onto people's plates, and hot parsley sauce can be poured over it.

St Joseph: 19 March

The spouse and protector of Mary, and foster father of the Christ-child. He was a carpenter, and took loving care of the Holy Family, teaching Jesus his own skills and trade. He is the patron saint of girls looking for a good husband! And, in an era when fatherhood is denigrated, he is a powerful intercessor on behalf of hard-working fathers seeking to cherish and protect their families and raise their children well.

In Italy – and in Italian-American parishes in the USA – St Joseph's Day is celebrated with a 'St Joseph's Table', on which are gradually stacked vast numbers of delicious sweets and pastries, all wrapped up and ready to be distributed: lollipops and chocolate bars and home-made cookies and goodies of all sorts.

It's also traditional to serve doughnuts on St Joseph's Day as a treat for the father of a family.

Lady Day: 25 March (The Annunciation)

As explained earlier, this is crucial to our understanding of the calendar. Lady Day is exactly nine months before Christmas and marks the day when Mary was told by an angel that she was to be mother of the Saviour. For centuries, this day – linked as it is to the spring equinox – was much honoured. It was effectively seen as the start of a new year, and indeed the new date was sometimes only used from 25 March rather than from 1 January as we do now. There is an old tradition that the first Good Friday fell on 25 March.

A herb much associated with Mary is the one that bears her name – rosemary. It blooms with blue flowers each spring. It is said to be very good for the hair: pick some sprigs of rosemary, and steep them overnight in hot water, and use this water to rinse your hair. Rosemary is said to be good for the memory – perhaps that is partly why Shakespeare has *Hamlet*'s Ophelia saying 'There's rosemary – that's for remembrance' and in some countries rosemary bushes are grown in cemeteries and there are posies of rosemary at funerals.

A big bunch of rosemary hung in the kitchen will help to keep flies away – and be usefully accessible when you want to use some dried rosemary for cooking.

Lenten sweets: 'Kwarisimal'

This is a tradition from Malta – sweets suitable for this season, using no eggs or fats.

Mix together

> Ground almonds
> Orange blossom water
> $1/4$ teaspoon of ground cinnamon
> Dried chopped fruit and mixed peel

Work these together and form them into small mounds, then bake for just a few minutes on a very low heat.

Laetere Sunday – Mothering Sunday

Lent can seem long. So, half-way through, we have a break. Its traditional name is Laetare Sunday – from the Latin for 'to rejoice'. It is the same root that gives us the old-fashioned girl's name Laetitia, shortened to 'Letty'. It was also sometimes called 'let up Sunday' because it was a day on which everyone could let up on their Lenten penances. Or it is simply mid-Lent Sunday.

As it was a holiday, people went home. Hence the tradition of Mothering Sunday – though this also comes from the references in today's liturgy to Jerusalem as the mother of us all, and to the Church as mother. One tradition is for people to go to their cathedral – the Mother church of the diocese – on this day. Another tradition is that of 'clypping the church' – everyone gathering round their parish church in a big circle, all holding hands, Auld Lang Syne-style, to show affection for the church.

Today many churches arrange for children to give flowers (usually daffodils) to their mothers, and indeed to all the ladies in the congregation, at the end of Mass.

The tradition of giving mothers a gift on this day was reinforced in the twentieth century: during the Second World War a great number of American soldiers and airmen came to Britain, and they brought with them the idea of the American Mothers' Day – which is in May. Befriended by British families, they repaid their hosts and hostesses with food and sweets and various luxuries from the USA – things which were in very short supply in wartime. Missing their own mothers, they gave to their 'adopted' British mums on Mothering Sunday the gifts they would give at home on Mothers' Day – flowers, chocolates, luxury foods.

The traditional gift from a daughter to her mother on Mothering

Sunday is Simnel Cake. This is also often eaten as an Easter cake. The name comes from the pounded ground almonds that make up the marzipan: in Latin, *similia*, the same root that gives us the Italian word 'semolina' for the grainy cereal that has the same texture.The pagan Romans had a festival, *Matronalia*, that celebrated motherhood and fertility at this time of year. With the coming of Christianity, motherhood was given a new dimension, dignity, and status, because Christ – the Son of God – was born of a mother, Mary.

Simnel Cake

    6 oz flour
    4 oz butter
    4 oz sugar
    6 oz currants
    2 oz mixed peel
    4 oz raisins
    4 oz sultanas
    2 eggs
    $1/4$ teaspoon grated nutmeg
    8 oz marzipan

Cream the butter and sugar until soft, add the eggs and then the flour and all the other ingredients except the marzipan. Line a large cake tin (both bottom and sides) with silver foil, and grease it thoroughly. Put half the cake mixture in, and then roll out the marzipan, and cut out a large circle of it. Place this on top of the cake mixture, and then put the remainder of the mixture on top. Bake in a moderate oven for 1 hour, then place some greaseproof paper on top and bake for a further forty minutes or until a knife inserted into it comes out clean.

To decorate: roll out the rest of the marzipan and cut out a circle. Spread the top of the cake with some melted jam and press the marzipan circle down on to it. Shape the rest of the marzipan into eleven balls – they represent the Apostles, minus the traitor Judas – and place these round the edge. You could write the word 'Simnel' in marzipan on top. It is traditional to brown the cake very, very lightly under a grill – giving the marzipan a gently bronzed look round the edges.

Holy Week

Palm Sunday

The most solemn and important week in the Christian calendar begins with Palm Sunday. Palm branches are blessed and distributed at church, and we hold them aloft in procession, just as people did so many years ago. Every donkey carries a cross on its back – marked plainly in its fur – and tradition says that this is because a donkey once carried the Saviour.

Palms are of course not grown in northern Europe, and the ones we use in church are imported. Traditionally, branches of pussy-willow or other spring branches have been substituted in processions.

Bringing home your palm from church, it can be tucked up behind a crucifix in one of the rooms, or you can fold it into a cross and tuck it into a prayer book or missal.

The Wednesday in Holy Week is traditionally called Spy Wednesday, because of the traitor Judas.

Holy Thursday (Maundy Thursday)

This is the day on which Christ celebrated the Last Supper – the first Mass, which was to culminate on Calvary. The name 'maundy' comes from the Latin *mandatum* – the same word which gives us the word 'command' and also words like 'mandate' and 'mandatory'.

The command which Christ gave us was the one that we should love one another, as he first loved us. In demonstration of this, he washed the feet of his disciples, and this is re-enacted every Maundy Thursday by the Pope in Rome, by each bishop in his cathedral church, and by many priests in their parishes, washing the feet of twelve men. It also used to be done by our monarch, and this tradition is still kept alive with the Royal Maundy, in which the Queen distributes money to as many elderly men and women as there are years of her reign. The ceremony is always held at some major cathedral in Britain. The Queen is preceded by someone carrying a nosegay – long ago, this was necessary because of the smell involved in washing the feet of the poor! The herbs in the nosegay – lavender, rosemary – are perhaps also reminiscent of the herbs that feature in the Passover meal. Lavender is also associated with spikenard, the oil poured over Christ's feet by the penitent woman in the gospel story. The Maundy money distributed by the Queen is specially minted and presented in attractive small red leather-covered boxes, bearing the Royal cipher. The coins often become family heirlooms.

The Last Supper was a Passover meal. The ritual for this is described in the reading from Exodus which we will hear at Mass this evening. An umblemished lamb or goat was eaten 'with unleavened bread and bitter herbs'.

Christ is our Passover Lamb. He was 'without blemish' and he died for us on the Cross. The drink that he was offered to alleviate his pain when he was on the Cross was the last ritual cup of the Passover meal, and he cried out 'It is finished'.

At the Maundy Mass, we will think of the Last Supper, and also of Christ's agony in the garden of Gethsemane. As Mass ends, the main altar is stripped and left bare, the Tabernacle door swinging open, candles blown out. The Blessed Sacrament is taken – in a procession, covered by a canopy and with altar servers bearing candles – to an Altar of Repose, where we can watch and pray with him. It is traditional to go from church to church visiting the Blessed Sacrament on this night, making seven visits in all.

Good Friday

This is the day of Christ's passion and death. It is a day of fasting, and abstaining from meat. The great commemoration in church of these events begins with the priest prostrating himself before the altar, and continues with the reading of the Passion, the veneration of the Cross, and Holy Communion.

Hot Cross Buns are the traditional food for this day. They are associated with fasting: this is a day when no meat is eaten, and not very much of anything else. Simple small buns marked with a cross symbolize what the day is all about. Over the years, the buns acquired dried fruit and spices and a glazed sugar top. (Now they are available in supermarkets all year round, which seems a pity, and makes today seem less special). Toasted and eaten for breakfast, they make the day seem important from the start.

How to mark Good Friday? Unless there is a film about Christ, or the relaying of a church service, it makes sense to switch the television off. Children can help to collect together items for the

Easter garden (see below), which makes a nice theme for a walk. There are also eggs to colour and decorate for Easter, and perhaps some Easter baskets to make. In addition to the main Good Friday service, there will be Stations of the Cross in church and perhaps a special children's service. Some families rent a suitable DVD of a film with a religious theme, or have a CD of a concert of sacred music.

In some parts of Europe, it is still traditional to put black crepe or black ribbon on the front door on this day, as for a funeral, and to wear dark clothes. There are also Good Friday processions, featuring people dressed up as characters showing the whole history of man's salvation: Adam and Eve, Abraham, Jonah (with his whale), Pontius Pilate, the women of Jerusalem, and so on. There are also penitents wearing dramatic hoods and carrying crosses, and banners bearing Christ's words from the Cross, etc.

In Malta one old tradition used to be that of carrying, from room to room around the house, a pan with the ashes made by the burning of the previous year's palms from Palm Sunday. The idea was to bless each room, and the pan would be swirled into corners, under beds, etc.

In German-speaking countries, Good Friday is called *Karfreitag* – from the same root as the English word 'care'.

It is traditional to drink no alcohol on Good Friday – because Christ went thirsty on the Cross. And, of course, fish is a traditional dish because no meat is eaten.

Any Good Friday meal will be a simple one. Try this Greek bean soup, served with warm crusty bread, or with garlic bread:

Greek Bean Soup

1lb dried white beans, or navy or pea beans; or lima beans or chick peas
3 quarts water
3 large onions, chopped
3 cloves garlic, minced
$1/2$ cup olive oil
1lb can of Italian peeled tomatoes
2 bay leaves
1 tablespoon fresh mint, chopped, or 1 teaspoon dried mint
Salt to taste

Pick over the beans, removing pebbles etc. Rinse. Bring the water to a boil, add the beans, and boil for 2 minutes. Remove them from the heat and let them sit for 1 hour.

In the meantime sauté the onions gently in the oil until translucent and golden. After the beans have soaked for an hour, add the onions, garlic, and the oil to the bean pot, along with the tomatoes, drained, pepper to taste, bay leaves, and half of the mint. Simmer, partly covered, until the beans are soft. You may wish to purée part or all of the soup in a blender. Thin it, if required, with juice from the tomato can, or water. Add the salt and the rest of the mint.

Variations: You can eliminate the tomatoes; use oregano or basil instead of mint; add chopped parsley at the end; or you can sauté some chopped celery along with the onion and garlic (Evelyn Birge Vitz, *A Continual Feast*).

The Bells on Good Friday

Church bells are not rung on Good Friday – no bells to summon people to services, no bells rung during any of the ceremonies – a rattle is used instead. An old legend says that, on the night of Good Friday, all the bells of churches across the world fly to Rome, where they are blessed by the Holy Father, and fly back again to their churches in time for the great Easter ceremonies that will start on Holy Saturday.

Easter Baskets

If you have saved some plastic bottles during Lent, now is the time to use them. Washing-up liquid bottles are best, but any other good-sized bottle that is not made of brittle plastic will do. First, wash them very thoroughly. Cut them off about three inches from the bottom: discard the top part. On the lower part, mark off dots half an inch apart. Using a ruler, draw a straight line down from each dot to the base. Now, with sharp scissors cut down the lines you have drawn. Now weave ribbon carefully in and out of the strips to make a basket. Stick down the end of the ribbon firmly before you begin – one way of doing this is to stitch it with a strong needle and thread. A strong stapler can also be used, or firm glue and then fasten it firmly when you have finished, too. Add a ribbon handle,

63

or one cut from the remainder of the bottle.

The baskets can now be filled with tissue paper and small chocolate or sugar eggs, a fluffy chick or two, some Easter biscuits, or any other goodies.

Holy Saturday

This is a day of preparation for Easter: there will be the Easter garden to prepare, and the house to clean and tidy for tomorrow's celebrations and visitors. There are Easter biscuits to bake, and perhaps an Easter branch to decorate for the breakfast table.

Coloured Eggs

There are various commercial dyes that turn eggs different colours, and these are fun to use – you can find them in craft shops or in the children's and stationery sections of large supermarkets. Mostly they are small pellets which dissolve in water, so you will need plenty of bowls to tackle the different colours. Some dyes come in kits with little stickers to use, too – bunnies and flowers and chicks and so on.

It is also possible to use natural dyes: try boiling up eggs with beetroot, which turns them a glowing pink, nettles, which turns them a dullish sort of green, or onion skins, which offer a sort of yellowish orange. Gently rubbing the eggshell with a paper towel dipped in cooking oil will give a nice sheen.

Alternatively, use crayons to draw faces on the eggs (but experiment first: some crayons are no use as the colour fades in water. Many felt-tip pens are useless for this reason too). A monk with a tonsure? A pirate with an eye-patch? A choirboy with his mouth a round 'O' with singing?

Hard-boiled eggs with shells that have been dyed are perfectly good to eat, and indeed can be enjoyed as part of a picnic on Easter Day or at Easter breakfast. But you may also like to have some eggs that are purely for decoration, and for this you need to blow the eggs: pierce them at each end (a hardware shop will sell you a small device that does this) and then blow the contents through. A beauty tip: you can then use the egg mixture, mixed with shampoo, for washing your hair, and it will give it extra bounce and shine.

The blown egg can then be painted and decorated in all sorts of ways, using paints bought from a craftshop. It is worth working out some designs on paper first.

An Easter Branch

Decorated blown eggs can hang from an Easter branch. Choose some nice twiggy branches with new leaves, and arrange them in a sturdy vase. Attach a length of cotton to each egg with strong sticky tape, and hang the eggs from the branch. This can make a centre piece for the Easter table.

An Easter Garden

Have a tray, or the lid of a biscuit tin, or a wide flat roasting-dish or similar. Collect moss to make a green lawn. In one corner you could make a pond: this could be a saucer of water surrounded by moss and pebbles, or it could be a small mirror. In another corner, make a mount: this is Calvary. Make a path of small neat pebbles leading up to it. On the top of the little hill, make three crosses of twigs bound with cotton (use purple thread if you have it). In another part of the garden have the tomb, built out of larger stones (usually one single stone for the back, and one for each side, with one flat one balanced across as a roof, is easiest). Seal the tomb with a stone at the front.

If you choose the right kind of dish, with adequate sides, and not too large, the Easter garden can travel quite successfully: it is nice to arrive with it on a visit to grandparents, where it will be much admired.

On Easter morning, the garden is transformed: drape golden ribbon over the main Cross on the hill, open up the tomb and lay a tiny scrap of white cloth, folded, inside, and plant daisies and celandines or other flowers in the moss.

Holy Saturday Evening

I am indebted to Helen Hull Hitchcock of Women for Faith and Family in the USA for this idea for the evening of Holy Saturday.

After supper, turn the oven on HIGH and leave it on. This is important – you have to do this before embarking on this project.

Then assemble the ingredients for the special Easter cookies:

Three eggs, with the whites separated from the yolks
1 teaspoon of vinegar
1 cup of water
1 cup of sugar
a little salt
1 cup of hazelnuts, almonds, or pecans
A Bible

Put the nuts in a stout plastic bag (or two bags, one inside the other) and let the children beat them with wooden spoons. Explain that, after Jesus was arrested, he was beaten by Roman soldiers. Read John 19:1–3.
    Let each child smell the vinegar. Put one teaspoonful into the mixing bowl. Explain that when Jesus was thirsty on the Cross, he was given vinegar to drink. Read John 19:28–30.
    Add the egg whites to the vinegar. Eggs represent life. Explain that Jesus gave his life for us. Read John 10:10–11.
    Sprinkle a little salt into each child's hand. Let them taste it. Sprinkle one pinch of salt into the mixing-bowl. Explain that this represents the salty tears shed by Jesus' followers, and our own sorrow for sin. Read Luke 23:27.
    Add one cup of sugar to the mixture. Explain that Jesus died because he loves us. He wants us to belong to him. Read Ps. 34:8 and John 3:16.
    Whip the whole mixture until stiff peaks are formed (or use a high-speed electric mixer). Explain that the colour white represents purity in God's eyes of those whose sins have been cleansed by Jesus. Read Isaiah 1:18 and John 3:1–3
    Fold in the broken nuts. Drop the mixture in teaspoonfuls on to a well-greased piece of oven-proof paper on a baking tray. Explain that each mound represents the rocky tomb where Jesus' body was laid.
    Put the whole batch in the oven and turn the oven OFF. Give each child a piece of sticky tape, and let them seal the door. Explain that Jesus' tomb was sealed. Read Matt 27:65–66.
    NOW GO TO BED! Explain that they may feel sad to leave the cookies in the oven overnight: Jesus' followers were in despair after he died. Read John 16:20 and 22.
    On Easter morning, when the oven is opened, give everyone a cookie. Notice the cracked surface and take a bite. The cookie is

empty! On the first Easter morning, Jesus' tomb was empty. Read Matt. 28:1–9.

The Easter Vigil

One of the most dramatic events the Church has to offer is the Easter vigil, beginning when darkness falls on Holy Saturday. We gather outside the church where the Easter fire is waiting. The great Paschal Candle will be lit from this, to the glad singing of *Lumen Christi!* and we will all light our own candles, filling the church with glorious light. Water will be blessed, which will be used for baptisms, and with which we too will be sprinkled as we renew our baptismal promises. When we emerge from the church having made our Easter Communion, Easter has begun: Christ is risen!

> I was born on Holy Saturday, April 16, 1927, in Marktl am Inn. The fact that my day of birth was the last day of Holy Week and the eve of Easter has always been noted in our family history. This was connected with the fact that I was baptized immediately on the morning of the day I was born with the water that had just been blessed. (At that time the solemn Easter Vigil was celebrated on the morning of Holy Saturday). To be the first person baptized with the new water was seen as a significant act of Providence. I have always been filled with thanksgiving for having had my life immersed in this way in the Easter mystery, since this could only be a sign of blessing. To be sure, it was not Easter Sunday but Holy Saturday, but, the more I reflect on it, the more this seems to be fitting for the nature of our human life: we are still awaiting Easter; we are not yet standing in the full light but walking towards it full of trust.
>
> Cardinal Joseph Ratzinger, now Pope Benedict XVI, *Milestones*

Easter

Easter Sunday

Christ the Lord is risen today
Alleluia!
Christians, haste your vows to pay
Alleluia!

Christ is risen! Easter is a day of celebration. In Poland, there is a tradition of taking the Easter breakfast – decorated eggs, freshly-baked rolls – to church in baskets to be blessed by the priest. In Britain, the custom of an Easter egg hunt is now widely established. Children hunt for eggs around the house and garden. I have never understood why there is a myth that the eggs are laid by a rabbit – it's daft, as rabbits don't lay eggs, and the Easter Rabbit is a modern concoction having only the most tenuous of connections with the Easter story. A much nicer link is the idea of Mary Magdalene seeking the risen Lord in the Garden, hunting here and there.

Miniature wrapped eggs – the very tiny kind, that are bought in packets, dozens at a time – are best for an egg-hunt. They are small enough to be hidden inside a daffodil, or perched, almost unseen, on the edge of a birdbath. You can even colour-code them, having one child look for pink eggs, one for silver, one for pale blue, and so on. Decorated baskets, or big paper cones covered with Easter pictures and symbols, can be distributed to be filled by the seekers.

The traditional dish for Easter lunch is roast lamb with garlic and rosemary: pierce the joint of meat all over and insert cloves of garlic and sprigs of rosemary, with more rosemary sprinkled on top. Rosemary can also be chopped up very finely indeed (children can help with this) and added to the gravy.

Many families eat a Christmas pudding, which has been maturing since December – this makes an enjoyable link with Christmas!

Cheesecake is a traditional Easter dish and involves lots of cream and eggs, very suitable after a Lenten fast.

In our family, a tradition has developed of having to complete word-searches before Easter eggs can be claimed. Everyone is given his or her own word-search – these are easy to concoct on a computer. You can personalize them: Granny has one with the names of flowers and gardening items, Auntie Joanna gets one filled with her favourite things like Chocolate Cake, Traditions, Bicycling, Embroidery, and Tea Time.

Eastertide

Easter lasts for forty days – until the Ascension, which was traditionally celebrated on a Thursday (in recent years, the Bishops of England and Wales decided it should be celebrated on the nearest Sunday). Eastertide is a time of celebration – there will be flowers in church (they have been absent throughout Lent) and hymns filled with *Alleluias* (a word we haven't heard at all in Lent) and a general sense of joy.

Ascension and Rogation

On the feast of the Ascension, we commemorate Christ's returning to his Father. The Scriptures give us an account of how the disciples accompanied Jesus to the Mount of Olives, and there, before their eyes, he rose heavenwards to the skies, and as they gazed and gazed, he disappeared from their sight.

> Men of Galilee, what are you wondering at, looking heavenwards? In the same way as you watched him going into heaven, he will come back. (Acts 1:11–12)

This has always been a great feast-day of the Church. The days immediately before the feast of the Ascension were traditionally known as 'Rogation days' from the Latin 'rogare' meaning 'to ask'. People were asking God for a blessing on the land, where the crops had been planted and were now beginning to sprout. Thus arose the tradition of walking in procession to bless the field. Old place names such as Gospel Oak remind us of this old tradition: at various set places the Gospel would be read or a psalm sung.

It is still a tradition to bless fields at this time of year, and in some seaside places there is a Blessing of the Sea, to ask God's protection on the harvest of fish.

It is perfectly possible to bless your own garden, or allotment, at Rogationtide. Invite a priest friend round to read the blessing and stay for supper. Or simply gather the whole family together and have the father of the family read out the blessing. Children enjoy planting simple things – like mustard and cress – that can be eaten. There is something immensely satisfying about seeing something grow day by day, and then enjoying eating it. A barbecue supper might be fun for Ascension Day – the first barbecue of summer.

Because the old Rogation processions were much enjoyed, they were not abandoned at the Reformation. People insisted on walking around the parish. So it was announced that the procession would be simply one of 'beating the bounds', so that people would know the parish borders. Some such ceremonies are still carried out. Do you know your parish boundary? Pack a picnic and a map and see if you can walk the parish boundaries on or near Ascension Day!

April Saints

St George: 23 April

The traditional Protector of the English realm has come back into fashion again recently, as his St George's cross has been adopted by the English football team. He was no mythical figure, but a real saint and martyr, who lived in the fourth century and was a high-ranking officer in the Roman Army in the Middle East in the reign of Diocletian. The Empire tolerated Christians as they were loyal, hard-working, devoted to the concepts such as tradition and honour, and had proved themselves courageous as soldiers and trustworthy in business and public life. But Diocletian wanted more. Christians believed in just one, true God – not a collection of idols with the Emperor at the heart of things. Finally recognizing that they were not to be budged, he issued a proclamation against them, their churches, funds, and property. Failure to comply would mean death. George boldly tore down the notice and was arrested. Subjected to hideous tortures, he refused to recant or deny his faith and was put to death. It was 23 April, 404, which happened to be Good Friday.

Hailed as a great and noble martyr, George's fame spread. There is evidence of early devotion to him in the ancient British Church, long before Augustine arrived in the sixth century to convert the invading Angles and Saxons. But he was particularly popular among the Christians of the Middle East, and it was here that, many centuries later, English soldiers fighting the Crusades encountered him. They brought back stories of how invoking his prayers had helped them in battle, and in due course the Crusaders' flag, the Flag of St George, became England's national flag and became incorporated into the Union Jack.

It would be worth celebrating St George's Day by wearing a red rose – his symbol – and having an English-themed supper, with singing of old English songs, recitation of some English poetry (Shakespeare, G. K. Chesterton, Keats, and some of Hilaire

71

Belloc's *Cautionary Verses*). Try boiled bacon and pease pudding, followed by a trifle with strawberry jelly, topped with whipped cream and decorated with red cherries to echo the colours of St George's Flag.

St Mark: 25 April

Matthew, Mark, Luke and John
Bless the bed that I lie on
Four corners to my bed
Four angels there be spread
One at the head, one at the feet
And two to guard me while I sleep
If any danger come to me
Sweet Jesus Christ deliver me.
If I should die before I wake
I pray the Lord my soul to take.

This ancient bedtime prayer evokes the four Evangelists, who wrote the Gospels. Mark is traditionally associated with the young man who sprints away naked in the Garden of Gethsemane.

St Mark is associated with the city of Venice, as his relics were brought there in the ninth century and a great church erected bearing his name.

Whitsun and Trinity Sunday

Pentecost – Whitsun

At Pentecost, we commemorate the coming of the Holy Spirit on the new young Church. The spirit appeared as tongues of fire. It is fifty days after Easter – *pente* is Greek for 'fifty'. It has its origins in a Jewish feast, held fifty days after Passover. This feast was all about thanking God for the fruits of the earth. This is still part of the Pentecost tradition, and we also thank God for his spiritual gifts.

The Gifts of the Holy Spirit are listed in the Catechism of the Catholic Church. There are seven of them. A way to remember this is that Pentecost is seven weeks after Easter. They are:

Wisdom
Understanding
Counsel
Fortitude
Knowledge
Piety
Fear of the Lord

The old English word for Pentecost is Whitsun. This commemorates the white robes worn by the newly-baptized in procession on this day.

The hedgerows are also white at this time of year, with May blossom and with 'Queen Anne's lace' or cow parsley.

In medieval times, white doves were sometimes released at church celebrations, for Whitsun, or showers of white rose petals were tossed at the congregation. Some churches even had a 'Holy Ghost hole' in the ceiling through which a great golden disc with a white dove painted in the centre would be lowered.

An outdoor picnic – perhaps with white meringues because it is Whitsun – is a good way to celebrate this weekend. It used to be a holiday weekend all over Europe, but increasing secularization means that public holidays sometimes coincide with church feasts and sometimes do not. This is an additional reason for making sure that we celebrate Whitsun properly in our families.

As there are seven Gifts of the Holy Spirit, why not seven different foods on the picnic? Or write the names of the Gifts on tiny slips of paper and wrap them up with sweets in tissue paper and bring a bagful along on a walk or to enjoy at the end of the picnic.

Trinity Sunday

Glory be to the Father
And to the Son
And to the Holy Spirit

The Sunday following Pentecost is Trinity Sunday. This honours the Blessed Trinity – Father, Son, and Holy Ghost – a most important doctrine to learn, because today it is very fashionable to say that Jesus Christ was a good man and maybe even a prophet, but not God's Son, one in being with the Father. We must counter this, and affirm the truth of Christ's Divinity.

St Patrick taught the Trinity using the shamrock leaf with its three parts. Sometimes the Trinity is symbolized by a triangle.

The Trinity is honoured in the names of churches, in Colleges at Oxford and Cambridge, in street names. We invoke the Trinity every time we make the Sign of the Cross. There are many old traditions connected with doing things in threes – because of the Trinity. That is why it is traditional to knock on a door three times – rat-tat-tat – instead of just once.

The Holy Family – Jesus, Mary, and Joseph, is also a reminder of the Trinity.

Corpus Christi: 'Trinity Thursday'

As the Last Supper took place on a Thursday, the Church has traditionally used this day of the week to honour the institution of the Eucharist and to thank God for Christ's presence among us in Holy Communion. The feast of Corpus Christi was appointed to be on the Thursday following Trinity Sunday. (Today in Britain it is now celebrated on the next Sunday.)

It is at this time of year that children make their First Holy

Communion, the girls in traditional white dresses. Corpus Christi processions are held, with a priest carrying the Eucharist in a monstrance beneath a canopy. It is traditional for children to walk in front, scattering rose petals to honour Christ's presence.

> *O Sacrament most holy*
> *O sacrament divine*
> *All praise and all thanksgiving*
> *Be every moment thine.*

The Visitation

On 31 May, the Church honours the Visitation – the day when Mary, according to the Scriptures, went to see her cousin Elizabeth, who like her was expecting a child. The feast of the Visitation thus falls between the Annunciation – when Mary learned that she was to be the mother of the Saviour, and that Elizabeth although past childbearing years was also with child – and the birthday of John the Baptist on 24 June.

Elizabeth's words on greeting Mary now form part of one of the most popular and well-loved prayers of all time, the Hail Mary, which opens with the words spoken to Mary by the Angel at the Annunciation. Mary responded with the Magnificat, a great hymn of praise to God.

> *Hail Mary, full of grace,*
> *The Lord is with thee*
> *Blessed art thou among women*
> *And blessed is the fruit of thy womb, Jesus*
> *Holy Mary, mother of God*
> *Pray for us sinners*
> *Now and at the hour of our death*
> *Amen.*

Magnificat

> *My soul proclaims the greatness of the Lord*
> *My spirit rejoices in God my Saviour;*
> *For he has looked with favour on his lowly handmaid*
> *And from henceforward all generations will call me blessed.*
> *The Almighty has done great things for me*
> *And holy is his name.*

He has mercy on those who fear him
From generation to generation.
He has shown the strength of his arm
And has scattered the proud in their conceit
He has cast down the mighty from their thrones
And raised up the lowly.
He has filled the hungry with good things
And sent the rich away empty.
He has come to the aid of Israel, his servant
Remembering his mercy and his promise
The promise he made to our fathers
To Abraham and his children for ever.

(Luke 1: 46–55)

Midsummer

St John the Baptist's Birthday

A happy holiday memory: up on an Austrian mountain, people gathered with music and delicious food around a bonfire. There was dancing and singing, tasty sausages followed by pastries and cream – and around us, on the other hilltops, we could see other fires. It was Midsummer night, the birthday of John the Baptist.

The tradition of lighting a bonfire on St John's Day is said to go back to the idea that Elizabeth lit a fire as a beacon to tell the news that her child, John the Baptist, had been born. In Ireland, the ashes of the 'St John's fire' are regarded as having a special quality, and are spread on the fields to ensure good crops.

Why don't we celebrate Midsummer in Britain? Our ancestors used to do so. Shakespeare wrote a whole play *A Midsummer Night's Dream* to celebrate it.

In medieval times, some of the original Christmas Nativity plays were in fact performed in midsummer, out of doors. People called 24 June the 'summer Christmas': it marks the birthday of St John the Baptist, cousin to Jesus Christ and herald of his coming. John the Baptist greeted Christ while they were both still in the womb. His birthday is exactly six months before Christmas, and is linked to the summer solstice, the longest day in the year. Christmas marks the winter solstice.

When Shakespeare wrote *A Midsummer Night's Dream* he deliberately incorporated some of the traditional Christmas themes: there is a donkey, for instance (remember Bottom the weaver, who suddenly acquires a donkey's head?), and there are a number of rustics, like shepherds. People expected some aspects of the Christmas story to be there, even just in a jokey way, to make the link.

A note for girls: an old tradition says that if you climb over nine fences, and also pick nine different kinds of flowers, on Midsummer's Eve, and then put the flowers under your pillow, you will dream of the man you will marry!

This is the right evening for an outdoor supper, over a bonfire or barbecue. Sit around late and long afterwards, and sing and talk.

Midsummer Lemonade for a hot day

Make this the day before a picnic, to take with you.

    2–3 lemons
    4 oz sugar
    1¹/₂ pints of water

Squeeze out the lemon juice into a jug. Stir the lemon rinds and the sugar into the boiling water. Leave this to cool, then strain it and add the lemon juice.

Midsummer games for long lazy afternoons with a picnic

'Animals'
The first person starts by naming an animal e.g. 'horse', and the next says an animal that starts with the last letter – 'elephant', and so on. If you can't think of an animal, you drop out. Winner is last one left in.

'I like lettuce'
(This was taught to me by my sister-in-law.) See how long it takes for people to catch on to what this game is all about. There must be two people who understand it to begin. One says 'I like lettuce but I don't like cucumber.' A follow-up could be 'I like cotton but I don't like rags.' Ask people to join in. They will be baffled, but someone will probably have a go: 'Um ... I like sandwiches but I don't like cake.' No good. They haven't got the point. So the initiator continues: 'I like cheese but I don't like yoghurt.' 'I like beef but I don't like lamb.' The solution is easy: the 'I like' bit refers to something with two letters together: the 'tt' in 'lettuce' and the 'ee' in cheese, contrasted with a word that doesn't have any double letters. Gradually, some people will catch on. Try it.

'Tennis-Elbow-Foot'

The first person says a word, any word. The next has to say one that is linked to it. The next must say a word that is linked again, but not linked to the first word. And the next person must make a link in a similar way, again not going back. Thus it could go: 'Tree – Christmas – cracker – biscuit – cooking – kitchen – .' See how long you can keep going.

'Stone/Paper/Scissors'

The old favourite. Two players sit opposite one another, hands behind their backs. They chant 'stone, paper, scissors' then produce one hand: it is either a stone (hand clenched in fist), scissors (fore-finger and neighbouring finger extended in scissor action) or paper (hand out open, flat palm). Scissors can cut paper, so scissors wins. Paper can wrap stone, so paper wins. Stone can blunt scissors so stone wins. This can be played indefinitely, or given a set number of turns, e.g. twenty.

Or play some Christmas games – 'Twenty Questions', 'Consequences', 'Word-and-Question' (see Christmas section).

For more energetic games for younger children, try 'Oranges and Lemons' (see under St Clement's Day in November) or other traditional singing games like 'The Farmer's in his Den':

Make a circle, and choose one child (boy) to stand in the middle. He's the farmer. All hold hands and walk round him singing:

The farmer's in his den
The farmer's in his den
Eee-ai-ee-ai
The farmer's in his den.

The farmer wants a wife
The farmer wants a wife
Eee-ai-ee-ai
The farmer wants a wife.
The 'farmer' chooses a girl who comes into the circle with him. Next you sing
'The wife wants a child ...'
'The child wants a dog ...'
Then when the dog has been chosen everyone rushes in to pat him or her, chanting

79

We all pat the dog
We all pat the dog
Eee-ai-ee-ai
We all pat the dog!

'Grandmother's Footsteps'

One person stands with his back to all the others, who are in a row
about ten yards from him. Object is to get to him and touch his
back without being seen. He can turn round at any instant, and
anyone he sees moving is out of the game.

A Scavenge Hunt

This works well on a summer day. Make a list beforehand of things
that children have to find (some of which will involve them making
things, too):

An acorn
Six stones or pebbles of the same size
A forked twig
A buttercup
A daisy chain
Three clover leaves
Something evergreen
Leaves from four different sorts of tree
A plait two inches long made from grass

Midsummer evening

Singing round the remains of a bonfire late on a summer night is a
good experience: try cheery songs like 'She'll be coming round the
mountain' and reflective ones like 'The Skye Boat Song'. Girl
Guide camp-fire evenings of this sort always ended with 'Taps',
sung to the tune of the Last Post:

Day is done
Gone the sun
From the sea, from the hills, from the sky
All is well! Safely rest!
God is nigh.

Saints and Feast-Days in Summer

St Peter and St Paul: 29 June

Peter was the Apostle to whom Christ said 'Feed my lambs – feed my sheep', and to whom he gave the 'keys of the kingdom of Heaven'. The symbol for St Peter is two crossed keys, and where you see statues of the Apostles, he is the one with the keys. There are some old inns around England called the 'Crossed Keys' and this is a reference to St Peter.

Because St Peter was the first among the Apostles – he is mentioned far more often than any other Apostle, always first, and usually in a leadership role – and because of the authority given him by Christ, we know him to be the first Pope. It is the tradition to pray for the Pope on this day.

On the island of Madeira, the fishing villages around the coast have special celebrations for St Peter's Day. A statue of St Peter – dressed as a pope – is carried in procession, and a great boat made out of wicker and decorated with fruit and flowers is created for him to sit in. As evening Mass ends, a feast with music and dancing, huge barbecues and plenty of local wine, begins, and people of all ages join in celebrations together.

> Peter's call to be a shepherd, which we heard in the Gospel, comes after the account of a miraculous catch of fish, after a night in which the disciples had let down their nets without success, they see the risen Lord on the shore. He tells them to let down their nets once more, and the nets become so full that they can hardly pull them in; they catch 153 large fish 'and although there were so many, the net was not torn' (John 21:11) This account, coming at the end of Jesus' earthly journey with his disciples, corresponds to an account found at the beginning: there, too the disciples had caught nothing the entire night; there, too, Jesus had invited Simon once more to put out into the deep. And Simon, who was not yet called Peter, gave the wonderful reply 'Master, at your word I will let down the nets'. And then came the conferral of his mission: 'Do not be afraid. Henceforth you will be catching men' Luke 5:1–11) . Today too the church and their successors of the apostles are told to put out into the deep sea of history and to let down the nets, so as to win men and women over to the gospel – to God, to Christ, to true life.
>
> Pope Benedict XVI,
> Inaugural Sermon, April 2005

In the nineteenth century, Cardinal Wiseman wrote a hymn invoking God's blessing on the Pope, and it was sung enthusiastically for many years. It fell out of favour as some of its lines began to sound somewhat out of date (referring to the speed of communication with the invention of the telegraph, they refer to 'the spark of unseen fire/that runs along the electric wire'). So, following the election of Pope Benedict XVI in 2005, two Catholic writers decided to honour the new Pope with a new version of the hymn. It keeps to the traditional opening line, and to Wiseman's original theme, which refers to pilgrims gathered in Rome and then to the worldwide Church, all praying for the successor of St Peter. Jeremy de Satge wrote new music specially for it. The tune is 'Holy Ghost, Balham'.

Full in the panting heart of Rome
The pilgrim's and the stranger's home
The voices rise to God in prayer
And ours with Christians gathered there.
God bless our Pope . . .
The great, the good.

Almighty God, whose sacred word
The great Apostle Peter heard
Who guides with ever-faithful hand
Your holy Church in every land.
God bless our Pope . . .
The great, the good.

O Lord of every age and place
Peter's successor asks your grace
Abundant faith and strength provide
Inspire and lead, protect and guide.
God bless our Pope . . .
The great, the good.

O God of light and God of truth
The hope of age, the strength of youth
To whom the holy martyrs pray
Renew and bless your Church today.
God bless our Pope . . .
The great, the good.

Where Peter is, the Church shall be
As Christ once taught in Galilee
Your saints join us to sing your praise
From now until the end of days.
God bless our Pope . . .
The great, the good.

Sometimes St Paul gets a bit neglected on his joint feast-day with St Peter. He is much honoured on the island of Malta where, of course, he was once shipwrecked.

> And when we had escaped, then we knew that the island was called Melita. But the barbarians showed us no small courtesy. For kindling a fire, they refreshed us all, because of the present rain, and the cold. And when Paul had gathered together a bundle of sticks, and had laid them on the fire, a viper, coming out of the heat, fastened on to his hand. And when the barbarians saw the beast hanging on to his hand, they said to one another: Undoubtedly this man is a murderer, who though he hath escaped the sea, yet vengeance doth not suffer him to live. And he indeed shaking off the beast into the fire, suffered no harm. But they supposed that he would begin to swell up, and that he would suddenly fall down and die. But expecting long, and seeing that there came no harm to him, changing their minds, they said he was a god. (Acts 28:1-6)

Malta has many statues of St Paul, usually showing him standing by a fire, and throwing a serpent into its flames. He is also always carrying a book of Epistles. On 29 June there are open-air gatherings with singing of folk songs. The traditional dish is stewed rabbit, with lots of wine.

St Swithin: 15 July

Swithin was Bishop of Winchester in the ninth century – before the Norman Conquest. At that time, England was divided into a number of different kingdoms and he was ruled by King Egbert of Wessex. He was appointed Bishop of Winchester in 852, and was a popular pastor, teacher, and ruler of the Church, living an austere and holy life. When he died ten years later he was buried, as he had wished, by the door of the church in a simple grave.

Later when the church was rebuilt, it was decided to give Swithin – whom all had regarded as a saint – a more splendid

83

grave up by the High Altar. The anniversary of his death, 15 July, was chosen for the ceremony and a great procession was formed. But the heavens opened and rain fell in torrents, drenching the monks carrying the relics, and all the bystanders. The great outdoor ceremonial had to be abandoned, and steady rain continued for a month. People said it was St Swithin, offended that his humble grave had been disturbed, refusing his grand new home.

Today, the tradition lingers: if it rains on St Swithin's Day it will be mostly wet weather for a full month afterwards. It is fun to keep a weather record to see if this old tradition holds good!

Rain on St Swithin's Day is actually felt to be a good thing by gardeners, especially those with fruit trees: the saying is 'St Swithin is blessing the little apples'.

The great abbey church at Winchester is well worth a visit. Jane Austen is buried there – it is now an Anglican cathedral.

St Benedict: 21 July

Benedict is the saint after whom the Benedictine rule – the basis of monastic life in Europe and the West – is named. He was born at the end of the fifth century. In 529 he established a monastery at Monte Cassino in Italy. The Benedictine Rule divides each day into eight hours of work, eight of prayer and eight of rest. This use of time, and the value given to manual work – previously seen as the work of slaves – transformed western culture.

It is to Benedictine monks that we owe a huge amount of our knowledge in many areas: agriculture, brewing of wine and ale, medicine, animal husbandry, art, music, architecture. It was Benedictine monks who created champagne, first named after one of their number – Dom Perignon (Benedictines are known as 'Dom'). Benedictines trained St Bernard dogs in the Alps to seek out and help lost travellers. They created the liqueur that still bears their name. They created the first Wensleydale cheese at their Yorkshire monasteries.

In England, all the monasteries were closed in the reign of Henry VIII. We can still see their ruins in our countryside, and visit them: at Tintern, Riveaulx, Jervaulx, Battle, and so many other places. The great abbey church at Westminster was left intact only because a king was buried there – Edward the Confessor – and Henry was wary of destroying so royal a monument – but the Benedictine monks, who had for hundreds of years farmed the land and created orchards and meadows where once there had been marshes (a nearby road is still called Abbey Orchard Street), were sent away.

Monastic life in Britain was revived in the nineteenth century. Today, there are communities of men and also communities of women living the Benedictine Rule at places like Farnborough in Hampshire, St Cecilia's and Quarr on the Isle of Wight, Minster in Kent, Downside in Somerset and Pluscarden in Scotland.

St Benedict's Day would be an excellent day on which to visit one of the great old ruined abbeys around Britain. Take a picnic lunch. In the ruins, look for the old refectory – where the monks would eat – and have your picnic there. It might also be appropriate to drink a glass of Benedictine . . .

St James: 25 July

This is a day to build a grotto! Long ago, those who wanted to go on pilgrimage to the great shrine of St James at Compostella in Spain would build small grottoes on street corners, and invite people to look at them, and leave a donation. The tradition lingered, and even into the twentieth century, London children would build grottoes: a simple layout of pebbles on the pavement, with, inside the border of stones, a candle, a couple of holy pictures, some flowers in a small jar, and a tin for pennies.

The story of the shrine in Spain is interesting. It is said that St James is buried there – at Finisterre, the very edge of what was then the known world, where he had earlier gone to preach. St James was, of course, one of the Apostles. His symbol is a cockle shell, and this has become the international symbol of pilgrims and travellers. Today, you can still walk the *Camino*, the ancient pilgrim route across France and Spain to Compostella, and arrive at the great church of St James, and greet the statue which every authentic pilgrim is meant to hug. Along the route, you will meet many other pilgrims, and you can stay at some of the old pilgrim hostels – or at various other places such as schools and church halls which offer help to genuine walking pilgrims.

You can also walk part of the pilgrim route in Britain – the old route down to the coast from London via Winchester can still be traced. Tradition says that yew trees always mark the pilgrim route.

St Anne and St Joachim: 26 July

They were the parents of Mary: the Scriptures do not give their names, but these have been passed down by long tradition. Anne is the same name as Hannah, and, like Hannah in the Old Testament, St Anne is said to have waited for a long time to have a child and to have been granted one in her later years.

St Anne is, of course, the grandmother of Christ and is therefore the patron saint of grandmothers. She is much honoured in Brittany, and the tradition was taken from there to Canada with the French settlers, so there is a shrine in Quebec.

'Nanna' – the name given to many grandmothers – derives from 'Anne'.

This is a day for visiting or telephoning grandmothers – who may also appreciate a handmade card with a message for St Anne's Day.

This is a time of year when all the fruit is getting ripe. A fruit pie is the traditional dish for this day. It would also be a good day to start the jam making. This is a traditional skill of grandmothers, and in late July the plums are starting to be ripe, and you may even find some early blackberries.

The flower we know today as 'Queen Anne's Lace' (cow parsley) was probably originally called 'St Anne's Lace', as it flourishes at this time of year.

Clafouti

This is a French fruit pie which is absolutely delicious. When learning the recipe from French friends over a glass of wine, we were interrupted by a Yorkshire girl who had lived for some years in France. 'Clafouti – oh, that's easy,' she told us. 'It's nowt but Yorkshire pudding wi' fruit in it.' Which is true, really.

2 eggs
5 oz flour
1/2 pint of milk
1/4 pint of cream
4 oz white sugar
Ripe plums or cherries, with the stones removed (other fruit that would be suitable could include apricots or blackberries)

Beat the eggs and fold in the flour and sugar adding the milk and cream and beating it to a smooth batter.

Grease a wide flat dish and place the fruit on the bottom, lying it flat. Pour the batter on top and bake in a moderate oven until the top is golden brown and the batter is firmly set. Serve hot or cold with thick whipped cream.

Fruit Picking and Jam Making

Going out to pick fruit is one of the satisfying things to do in summer, and you don't have to live in the country to do it. You will find blackberries growing in parks and on the local Common, in cemeteries (look along the hedge, especially if it is overgrown) and in all sorts of odd places. Take a picnic, and some kitchen wipes for sore and sticky fingers. Take lots of plastic bags (place one inside the other – blackberries can get heavy and it is heartbreaking if the bag splits!).

Kitchen wipes, Eau de Cologne, or lavender oil are all good for nettle stings (it's very annoying, but the most luscious blackberries are often found near clumps of nettles).

To Make Blackberry Jam

Put the fruit in a colander and run lots of cold water over it. Be sure to remove any bits of twig – and any small spiders!

Weigh the fruit – and, remembering how much it weighs, put it in a big saucepan and bring it to the boil. You do not need to add any more water. Keep stirring: the fruit will go mushy and form a rich pulpy liquid. Cook until all the berries are soft. The mixture will bubble and spit: you will need to wear a pinafore, and to clean the top of the oven afterwards.

Now add the sugar – a pound of sugar for each pound of fruit. Keep stirring until the mixture 'wrinkles' on top. The best way to test if the jam is ready is to place a spoonful in a saucer, let it cool, and see if it has a skin on top and is almost setting.

Heat lots of clean jam jars in the oven. Lift them out CARE-FULLY, wearing oven gloves. Pour the jam mixture into the jars. Seal the tops: you do not need elaborate tops for this, but circles cut from clean plastic bags, and held in place by rubber bands, will do very well.

If you do not heat the jam jars, they will crack and all your work will be wasted.

Jam making is not suitable for children, but they can enjoy making jam labels. These can be hand-written or produced on a computer. They should include the date 'Plum Jam, 2006' but it's nice to add the saint's day too. If you are planning to sell the jam at a church fete or similar, you could add something like 'Specially produced for St Joseph's Church Fete, August 2007' or whatever.

Children can also help to cut out circles from pretty cotton or gingham and put them in place with elastic bands or tightly-drawn ribbon over the tops of the jars when the jam is cooled. Make the circles generous – enough to have a good inch or so sticking out as a frill when the circle is placed over the jam jar. Cutting round the edge with pinking shears helps prevent fraying and looks pretty.

You do not need to buy special material: keep a scrap bag and use material from old cotton blouses or shirts, well washed. Iron the circles before placing them on the jam jars.

Preserving Fruit

Blackberries and raspberries will freeze well – just wash the fruit in water and pack it into plastic bags, seal them and put them in the freezer.

You can also bottle blackberries very easily: after washing the fruit, pack it into clean jam jars, and then place these in the oven, with foil over the tops so the fruit does not burn. Leave in a moderate oven until the fruit has gone well down in the jars, is bubbling and is lighter in colour.

Meanwhile, mix a syrup: one pound of sugar to half a pint of water. Bring to the boil and stir till the sugar dissolves. Do not let it burn! Transfer to a jug while still hot (warm the jug first to avoid cracking) and pour the syrup into the jars. To seal them, you can use rounds cut from plastic bags and ordinary rubber bands, as with jam making. You will need to wear oven-gloves and be very deft. Work slowly and carefully as everything is very hot. The berries thus preserved will last all winter. You will want to use some for blackberry and apple pie at Michaelmas.

The Assumption: 15 August

Called the 'Dormition' in the Eastern Church, this feast honours the day when Mary, mother of our Saviour, was taken up to Heaven body and soul.

It's a day for going bathing or paddling! An old Irish saying is that 'There's a blessing in the water' on the feast of the Assumption. Make it a day by the sea, have a paddling pool in the garden, or take the family to a swimming pool!

The idea of there being 'a blessing in the water' may also be behind the tradition of *Dydd Iau Mawr* (Great Thursday) in the Welsh town of Aberporth. On the second Thursday in August, there was a general exodus to the beach, where everyone enjoyed a bathe and a picnic. Miners took a day off work in order to be there. In the 1920s, the custom was so popular that 8,000 people were calculated to be present. In addition to enjoying themselves on the beach, people went to concerts in the village hall – later moved to the Welfare Park because of the numbers – and took part in fancy dress parades, cricket, pony rides, and clay pigeon shooting. The custom started to disappear at one stage, but was revived in 1992. Although today there is no reference at all to the Assumption in the festivities, the origins of this time of celebration seem to go back to a distant past, and may well be pre-Reformation.

> Now in Heaven, a great sign appeared: a woman, adorned with the sun, with the moon under her feet, and around her head a crown of twelve stars. (Rev 12:1–7)

St Bartholomew: 24 August

One of the Apostles, St Bartholomew is usually identified with Nathaniel, whom Christ praised for having an open and simple heart. Bartholomew is said to have preached the Gospel in India and in Armenia, where he was martyred.

> Jesus went out on to the mountain-side, and passed the whole night offering prayer to God, and when the day dawned, he called his disciples to him, choosing out twelve of them; these he called his apostles. Their names were: Simon, whom he also called Peter, his brother Andrew, James and John, Philip and Bartholomew, Matthew

and Thomas, James the son of Alphaeus, and Simon who is called the Zealot, Jude the brother of James, and Judas Iscariot, who betrayed him. (Luke 6:12–19)

St Bartholomew was a popular saint in medieval times, and the great hospital in London, known colloquially as Barts, is of course named after him. It was founded in the twelfth century, almost a thousand years before the National Health Service, and has been providing a service to London's sick people ever since.

His feast-day was known as Bartlemas. Especially popular at the annual Bartlemas Fair were apples on sticks, drenched in honey – an idea we still enjoy today as the toffee-apple.

Honey Toffee-Apples

Choose good, fresh, juicy apples with no maggots or blemishes. Have some metal skewers or sharp-pointed sticks to push into them – they must go in firmly so that the apple can be held while eating. Some supermarkets and hardware stores market skewers for barbecueing – these would be ideal. Wash the apples but do not peel them.

I got this recipe for 'Honey Toffee' from *Festivals, Family, and Food* by Diana Carey and Judy Large (a warmly recommended book). They suggest it simply as an enjoyable sweet in its own right, but it would be ideal to make toffee-apples.

> Boil 10 oz of butter and 4 oz of pure honey with a quarter of a pint of water. Boil to 114–118 degrees (238–245°F) (when you place a little in cold water it will form a soft ball). Pour on to a greased tin, then cut the toffee into small squares before it sets.
>
> To use the toffee for apples, simply leave it in the pan, then dip the fruit in this mixture and leave to set on a tray lined with sheets from a plastic bag. Pour any mixture left over into a tin as directed above. It can be wrapped in greaseproof or cellophane paper when cut up.

The authors add 'This is very good for colds'.

Our Lady's Birthday: 8 September (Marymas)

This marks the end of the summer harvesting. Long ago, this was the date on which all harvesting on the common fields owned by the feudal lord was deemed to be completed. Peasants could then work on their own small garden plots, where they grew herbs and useful vegetables. To mark the day, there was a great feast, and everyone took a holiday.

Mary has always been seen as the patron of the home and family, the domestic scene. She has always had an association with gardens, herbs, and flowers. So many are named after her: for example, marigolds, lady's tresses.

Rosemary Bread

To celebrate harvest-time, and to honour Mary, why not bake some harvest rolls, flavoured with rosemary, which bears her name?

    1 sachet dried yeast
    1¹/2lbs of white flour
    1 oz butter or margarine
    Cup of warm water
    Some rosemary, cut and pounded until it is almost powder

Work the butter into the flour, then add the yeast and work the mixture to a paste with the warm water. Knead it on a floured board for a good 5 minutes, then leave it to rise in a bowl covered with a clean cloth, in a warm place, for an hour. Knead it again and divide it into rolls. Place on a greased pan about 2 inches apart. Leave again, covered, for 20 minutes – the mixture should almost double in size. Sprinkle the rosemary on top. Bake in a moderate oven until golden-brown. They should make a hollow noise when tapped.

Serve warm, with lots of butter, with soup for supper.

Autumn

Season of mists and mellow fruitfulness
Close bosom-friend of the maturing sun
Conspiring with him how to load and bless
With fruit the vines that round the thatch-eaves run
John Keats

This is my favourite season of the year, when the harsh heat of summer abates, and all sorts of activities start up again after the July/August break.

Saints and Feast-Days in Autumn

St Michael and other Archangels: 29 September (Michaelmas)

Long ago, Lammas on 1 August marked the start of the summer's harvesting with a Loaf Mass. Michaelmas – the feast of St Michael on 29 September – marked its ending, with a big thanksgiving celebration.

We don't seem to say 'thank you' very much to God these days – we take food for granted, complain about it when it isn't exactly to our liking ('I couldn't get any slimline lychee juice, or avocado mousse – this supermarket is hopeless!'), we throw lots of it away, eat huge quantities of junk food and snacks in the street or while watching television, and have a massive obesity crisis through overeating. Many children probably don't know that bread comes from flour which comes from wheat, which has to be grown and harvested. Very few are given the chance to try their own hand at growing a row of beans or a patch of lettuces.

September and Michaelmas are a time to thank God for our food. The old tradition was to eat a roasted goose – the Michaelmas goose, which had been fattened up on the gleanings of corn at the end of harvesting. It was sometimes stuffed with chopped raw apple before cooking, to give a tender and sweet taste to the meat.

92

Another Michaelmas tradition is apple pie, or (better still, in my opinion), blackberry and apple crumble, served with thick cream.

Tradition says that blackberries cannot be picked after 29 September, because the devil spits on them at Michaelmas because of his anger at being cast out of Heaven. It is certainly true that the berries are musty and inedible by the end of September.

Michaelmas is a quarter day – the Autumn equivalent of Lady Day in March. It was traditionally a day when rent was paid. In some parts of Europe, it was also a day when contracts of summer work ended, and people could hire themselves out for the coming winter season.

Why not invite family and friends together for a Harvest supper – roast chicken served with apple sauce, home-baked bread rolls, and a blackberry and apple pie with fruit you have picked yourselves?

Make apple jelly to enjoy all winter, and to give away as Christmas gifts: wash, peel and roughly chop up plenty of apples, and boil them up with water until soft. Strain this liquid through muslin so that it drips into a bowl. The easiest way to do this is to make a jelly-bag: a square (about 6 inches square) of muslin or some other thin cotton material, with a long tape sewn at each corner. Upend a kitchen stool, and tie the tapes round each leg. Place a bowl underneath, on the upended seat of the stool. Now pile the apple mixture into the cotton square and let it drip through all day.

Measure up the liquid and then boil it up with sugar as for jam, using a pound of sugar for each pint of juice. Proceed as for jam making (see under 'St Anne's Day').The apple juice and sugar will slowly turn from pale green to amber as you stir.

A jar of home-made apple jelly – with a pretty cotton top tied with ribbon, and a label stating that it was made at Michaelmas – makes a very attractive gift. Apple jelly is excellent with roast pork, or with boiled bacon, or with chicken, and of course is delicious simply spread on buttered toast.

St Francis of Assisi: 4 October

This much-loved saint was the son of a wealthy merchant, born in Porziuncola in the thirteenth century – his name *Francesco* was a nickname because his mother was French so his friends called him 'little Frenchy'. After a carefree life with other well-to-do young men, he underwent a dramatic conversion experience and vowed himself to God's service. In prayer, he seemed to hear an image of Christ, calling from a crucifix in the church of San Damiano, saying 'Rebuild my church' and he took this message literally, building a new church there with his own hands. Disowned by his father, who felt he had humiliated the family, he gathered companions and went to Rome where they sought permission from the Pope to establish a new religious community which became one of the great Orders of the Church, the Franciscans.

In popular culture, St Francis has become the 'patron saint of animals' because of his approach to nature – loving the simple, everyday things provided by God and being grateful for them. His feast-day, along with that of St Leonard, is thus associated with the blessing of animals. He is also patron saint of the 'green movement', and of all those concerned with ecology. A day for arranging a clean-up job at some local beauty spot? Turn up with plenty of bin-bags and – wearing rubber gloves – pick up litter and take it to a dump. Cleaning up a local stretch of river, or beach, will be much appreciated too. Larger items of rubbish – furniture, electrical appliances – can be removed by a local authority, so find out the relevant telephone numbers (use the Internet). A team of friends can get involved with this – or why not a local youth group, Confirmation class, or similar?

St Leonard: 6 October

He is the patron saint of horses and of riders, and of domesticated animals generally. You will find little shrines to him along the country paths and bridleways of Germany and Austria. He was much venerated in medieval England and there are a number of old churches named after him. This is a traditional day for blessing stables, or for blessing domestic pets – cats and puppies and rabbits. Some churches have services for children in which pets (at least, those which are in some way portable!) are brought for blessing.

Not much is actually known about the life of St Leonard, but he is said to have been a hermit – and presumably to have made friends with animals, much as St Francis of Assisi is said to have done.

Our Lady of the Rosary: 7 October

This feast-day has given rise to the tradition of marking, in the Catholic Church, the whole of the month of October as a month dedicated to that ancient prayer, the Rosary. During the period of the Reformation, when Europe was divided because of Catholic/Protestant conflict, a new threat arose from militant Islam. A great sea battle was fought at Lepanto on 7 October 1571 and the victory of the Christian fleet under Don John of Austria was attributed to the thousands of people in various prayer-groups across Europe praying the Rosary. Initially called Our Lady of Victory, today's feast was established by Pope Pius V. The name was changed to Our Lady of the Rosary by Pope Gregory XIII.

If you do not have a rosary, or do not know how to use one, then this is the day on which to get started. Pope John Paul II renewed interest among Catholics in the Rosary, adding a further set of Mysteries – the Mysteries of Light – to those already honoured for centuries, the Joyful, Sorrowful, and Glorious Mysteries, all commemorating events in the life of Christ and the unfolding drama of our salvation.

The Rosary

The Joyful Mysteries
The Annunciation, The Visitation, The Nativity, The Presentation, the Finding of Christ in the Temple.

The Luminous Mysteries
The Baptism of Christ by John the Baptist, The Wedding at Cana, Christ Preaches the Coming of the Kingdom, The Transfiguration, and the Institution of the Eucharist.

The Sorrowful Mysteries
The Agony in the Garden, the Scourging at the Pillar, the Crowning with Thorns, the Carrying of the Cross, the Crucifixion.

The Glorious Mysteries
The Resurrection, the Ascension, the Descent of the Holy Spirit, the Assumption, the Crowning of Mary in Heaven and the Glory of all the Saints.

St Edward the Confessor: 13 October

If you are a Londoner, today is a day to visit Westminster Abbey! It was built by Edward the Confessor, our last Saxon king before the Norman Conquest. And he is buried there – when all the great shrines of England were destroyed under Henry VIII, the tomb of St Edward the Confessor remained intact – Henry felt that destroying a royal tomb might give people ideas, so he arranged that it be left just as it was.

The Angles and Saxons, originally fierce pagan interlopers in Britain, were evangelized in their turn by Augustine and his band of monks, sent by Pope Gregory in 497. By the time Edward inherited the throne in the tenth century, there were many Saxon saints. The nation had been united from its seven kingdoms (the heptarchy) in the year 800 under King Egbert, who inherited the throne while on his way to Rome on pilgrimage. Under Edward the Confessor, the nation had over twenty years of peace. The king was known for his kindness to the poor, and his sense of justice. He built a number of churches, and co-ordinated much of the legal system under 'King Edward's Laws'.

The Benedictine monks at Westminster drained the land of what was originally Thorney Island on a marshy bend of the Thames. Under the protection of the Abbey, Parliament met and it continues to meet on the same spot.

A tip: if you want to visit Westminster Abbey and your intention is to pray, you do not need to queue up with all the paying visitors. Simply go to the main door, the West Door, and explain to the functionaries there that you want to enter for the purpose of prayer – they will wave you in, and direct you to a small chapel on your right, just near the Tomb of the Unknown Warrior. This is reserved for private prayer.

On your way, you will also be able to view the whole of the nave, looking up towards the sanctuary and the High Altar. St Edward's tomb is up there in the chancel, beyond the screen.

St Luke: 18 October

St Luke was one of the four Evangelists. He was a Greek, and tradition says that he was a doctor of medicine. He has long been patron saint of the medical profession.

St Luke's Gospel gives us the most detailed descriptions that we have of the Annunciation and of Christ's birth – prompting the thought that he obtained his information directly from the Virgin Mary. Luke travelled with St Paul on some of his missionary journeys, and went with him to Rome.

St Luke's Day, falling in mid-October, comes at a time when the weather is neither very hot not very cold, giving us the expression 'luke-warm'.

St Simon and St Jude: 28 October

The Lord Mayor of London is always inaugurated with a big procession – the Lord Mayor's Parade – at this time of year, and this is because, long ago, he was always elected to take office on the feast of Saints Simon and Jude.

Both were Apostles. In statues, St Simon is usually depicted with a saw – he is said to have been martyred by being killed with a saw – and St Jude with an architect's square, because he was a 'builder of the house of God'. They were cousins of Christ, and it is possible that they worked in the same profession in which he was trained, as carpenters and craftsmen.

St Jude – for reasons that I have never been able to discover – is the patron saint of 'hopeless cases', and has for this reason always been very popular. There is a tradition that, if you pray for St Jude's help and your prayer is granted, you make this known – and this in recent years has come to mean, specifically, that you place an advertisement in a Catholic newspaper thanking him!

Hallowe'en – All Saints – All Souls

31 October, 1 November, 2 November

Today Hallowe'en, on 31 October, is a big commercial matter. Plastic pumpkins, masks, witches' hats – and all the paraphernalia of children's parties with entertainers, paper napkins, novelty gifts, and the rest – are on sale. The tradition of 'guising', going from house to house dressed up in old clothes and acting out plays or telling jokes – crossed the Atlantic and merged with the tradition of 'mischief night' (in which people unhinged gates, overturned

rubbish, emptied water-butts, or caused other nuisances to neighbours) to become 'trick or treat' in America. In the late twentieth
century it thus returned to Britain and now children dress up as
ghosts and ghouls and walk down suburban streets to knock on
doors and get sweets.

An anti-Hallowe'en campaign has also started, with various
groups of people creating an informal alliance – Christians, who
feel the ghosts-and-ghouls bit has gone rather too far, and parents
who are tired of having to buy lots of expensive plastic gimmicks,
or who would rather their children didn't walk around the streets
in the dark visiting strange houses.

What does 'Hallowe'en' really mean? The word simply means
'All Hallow's Eve' – the Eve of All Hallows, All Saints. The feast
of All Saints is on 1 November; Hallowe'en is the evening before,
31 October. We still use the word 'hallowed' meaning 'holy'. It is
part of the Lord's Prayer: 'Hallowed be thy name', and we sometimes speak of a holy place – a monument to the war dead, an
ancient cathedral – as being 'hallowed ground'.

Traditionally, the Eve of All Saints was regarded as a 'spooky'
time for a variety of reasons: the darkness is gathering as
November arrives, it was the time of year when our pagan ancestors remembered their dead and associated death with autumn and
the dying of the trees and flowers, and November was the month
set aside by the Church for prayer for the dead. The great Feast of
All Saints was, in medieval times, celebrated with bonfires – the
origins of our November bonfire tradition, which certainly predates
Guy Fawkes. And it was assumed that Satan was angry at the
thought of all those saints in Heaven – so this was a night when
witches swooped around the sky on broomsticks, spells were
chanted, and occult things occurred.

There is undoubtedly a renewed interest in paganism and the
occult at the present time, so undue enthusiasm for 'spooky' things
at Hallowe'en does seem rather unhelpful. Some churches try to
arrange their own events, with all the trimmings of an old-fashioned
Hallowe'en party and none of the spookiness. Sometimes they
invite children to come dressed as saints, and have a lantern-lit
parade, and this works quite well.

Certainly the right way to celebrate Hallowe'en is with attractive
traditions that emphasize the link with All Saints.

There could be games such as:

apple-bobbing – just apples in a bucket of water, and you have to grab one with your teeth, while your hands are firmly behind your back.

tastes – blindfold, you are given a teaspoonful of something to eat and you have to say what it is – it's amazing how simple things like milk, sugar, butter, olive oil, or honey are hard to identify!

blindfold feeding – blindfold two people, sit them opposite each other with bowls of cereal and have them try to feed each other. Pointless and hilarious.

Traditional food is parkin (sticky dark gingerbread), hot punch, sausages, baked potatoes and – a recent arrival via America – pumpkin pie. Pumpkins are now on sale everywhere at this time of year, and in addition to using some of the pulp to make a pie, you can use the rest to make soup. Having scooped out the centre of the pumpkin and sliced out flesh that you need, you turn the shell into a pumpkin lantern by cutting a wide curved slit for a smiling mouth, and squares for the eyes and nose. A small flat candle inside completes the job.

More traditional in Britain is a turnip lantern – smaller, and tougher to make because the pulp of the vegetable is more resistant to a knife.

A pumpkin or turnip lantern can be left glowing on the doorstep as a decoration or used as a centerpiece for a party table, or carried round if there is to be a procession.

All Saints

This is a major feast-day of the Church, and a day on which we recall all the saints in Heaven. A good day to find out about any saints whose names we bear in the family – not only our first names, but also other names, including Confirmation names. It is interesting to look for symbols of saints in old churches: a figure with half a cloak is St Martin, crossed keys means St Peter, a shell means St James, a lily is often St Joseph – who may also often be shown with his carpentry tools – martyrs always carry a palm, and so on. Note that the figures on either side of Christ on an old rood screen (rood is the ancient name for a cross) are Mary and St John, while a figure kneeling at the foot and weeping is Mary Magdalene. Armed with knowledge gained from the Internet, the local library, and bookshops, (*The Penguin Dictionary of Saints* is excellent), children can learn how to 'read' an old church so that pictures, statues, and stained glass come to mean something.

All Souls

On All Souls Day, 2 November, we remember the dead, and pray for them. It is a tradition to visit a family grave on this day, and leave a candle or flowers there after saying a prayer.

The traditional prayer for the dead is very consoling:

Eternal rest grant unto them, O Lord
And let perpetual light shine upon them,
Amen.

It is also traditional to say the '*De Profundis*' Psalm:

Out of the depths I cry to Thee, O Lord
Lord, hear my voice
Let thine ear be attentive
To the voice of my pleading
If thou, O Lord, shalt observe iniquities,
Lord, who shall endure it?
But with Thee there is merciful forgiveness
And by reason of Thy law I have waited for Thee, O Lord.
My soul hath relied on his word; my soul hath hoped in the Lord
From the morning watch, even until night
Let Israel hope in the Lord.
Because with the Lord there is mercy
And with him fullness of redemption
And he shall redeem Israel from all its iniquities.

(Ps. 129)

Long ago, children used to go from house to house, offering to say a prayer for anyone from the household who had died that year, and in return would receive a 'soul cake', a flat fruit bun. (This is obviously also linked with the tradition that gave us the modern 'trick or treat'.)

100

Soul Cakes

2 oz butter
2 oz white sugar
4 oz white self-raising flour
1 cup each of currants and raisins
1 egg
$1/_2$ teaspoonful of mixed spice
Milk to mix

Cream together the butter and sugar, beat in the egg and fold in the flour, mixed spice, and dried fruit. Spoon into well-greased patty-pans or paper cake-cups and bake for 15 minutes in a moderate oven. Serve warm at tea-time – and don't forget to pray beforehand.

St Martin: 11 November (Martinmas)

He was a Roman soldier, born in the early part of the fourth century in what is now Hungary, and legend says that one night as he was walking home, clad in his warm regulation cloak, he saw a beggar shivering by the roadside, and, taking pity on him, slashed his cloak in half with his great sword, and gave him half. Then, still clad in regulation uniform, he made his way home. That night, Christ appeared to him in a vision, wearing the half cloak: 'Inasmuch as you have done it to the least of my brethren, you have done it to me.' Martin became a convinced Christian and was baptized. He lived for a while as a hermit, becoming a missionary preacher and eventually Bishop of Tours in what is now France. He evangelized widely, lived simply, taught well, and was much loved. He lacked any personal ambition and was known always to put the needs of the Church first. He had accepted the role of bishop only very reluctantly.

His popularity was such that he was widely acclaimed as a saint – he is one of the first notable Christians of the early centuries who, while not a martyr, was officially declared a saint.

Because of his popularity in France, the French insisted that the Armistice which concluded the First World War be signed on his feast-day, which was partly why 11 November was chosen.

In many parts of Europe, children honour St Martin's Day by walking out in the darkening evening with big paper lanterns.

These are fun to make and should be carried on the end of a long stick.

You will need:

A wide strip (6 to 8 inches wide, and about 18 inches long) of strong paper
A large square piece of the same paper, approx 1 foot square
Blue or red tissue paper
Glue and sticky tape
A small 'night light' candle in its metal container
String

Roll out the paper and cut some windows in it (plan these carefully first). Some could be star shaped: make these by drawing two triangles, one overlapping the other at right-angles. Glue red or blue tissue paper over these windows. Bend the paper round into a circle and tape the edges together

Make a base for your lantern out of paper: stand your basic lantern on the square sheet of paper and cut a generous circle round it. Draw a smaller circle within this that is the exact size of your lantern. Turn up the edges around this smaller circle Place this circular sheet inside your lantern and glue in firmly in place. Glue a small night light on to this base.

Make a long handle for your lantern with string. It will be hot to hold. It is best carried by being fastened to a stick which is then held out horizontally, fishing-rod style.

Light the candle inside with a long taper. Take the children on a long lantern-walk through the nearby streets, and home to hot chocolate and pastries.

Remembrance Day

The eleventh hour of the eleventh day of the eleventh month – the awesome silence of Remembrance Day when people gather to honour the war dead is deeply etched into our national consciousness.

The First World War was initially called simply the Great War. When it began in 1914, people were still thinking in nineteenth-century terms – bright uniforms, Royal dynasties, deep national convictions and tribal loyalties, soldiers on galloping horses, bugle calls across wide open battlefields. But it was not to be like that at all. For four grim years, young men from across Europe, and from Australia, New Zealand, Canada, and elsewhere fought in horrible conditions, enduring lice, wounds, the prospect of hideous disfigurement, hunger and thirst, and bitter cold. Millions died. When it finally ended with the Armistice which would take effect at 11 a.m. on 11 November, families across the world grieved for sons and brothers, husbands and sweethearts. For many women, all prospects of marriage and children were gone, and a lonely and hard-working life loomed, caring for elderly parents without the support of husband or brother. A whole generation of young men – including those who would have been among the national community's natural leaders – had perished. Many people would now live in poverty because of the economic chaos created by the war. In Russia, wartime events had allowed the Bolsheviks to grab power and Communism was to cause famine, hunger, and denial of freedom for millions for decades. Across Europe, as monarchies crumbled and new nation states were announced, power vacuums emerged and new tensions arose. The scene was steadily set for another war, and in 1939 the Second World War began.

On Remembrance Day, we remember the dead of the two World Wars, honour their courage, and wear poppies commemorating those that bloomed in the Flanders battlefields of the First World War.

It is an extraordinary turn of history that gave us this Remembrance Day in November – the very month which for centuries had been honoured by all of Christendom as the month of prayer for the dead. The very words 'November' and 'Remembrance' go together in people's minds, and the splash of red on a dark overcoat in November gloom as a poppy is pinned on, is one of the most evocative of national images.

> *They shall grow not old, as we who are left grow old.*
> *Age shall not weary them, nor the years condemn.*
> *At the going down of the sun and in the morning*
> *We will remember them.*
>
> Laurence Binyon (1869–1943),
> 'For the Fallen' (1914)

St Clement: 23 November

He was the third Pope after St Peter, and he was martyred by having an anchor tied around his neck and being thrown into the river Tiber in Rome. He is traditionally the patron saint of blacksmiths – because they were the manufacturers of anchors. Blacksmiths would make sparks with gunpowder on their forges on his feast-day – another link with our modern November fireworks. In some districts, there was a celebration feast for blacksmiths on St Clement's Day, with someone dressed up as 'Old Clem' in a battered hat and with a pipe, acting as host and welcoming everyone at the door.

The children's rhyme 'Oranges and Lemons' is said to refer to the citrus fruits being unloaded at London's docks. It certainly refers to all the old churches of London, each district with its own characteristic: the grim reference to justice from the Old Bailey, the perkiness of Hackney, and so on. The rhyme, now a pleasant singing-game, has its origins in the fact that all the bells of Old London would ring solemnly when someone was being taken for execution.

You sing the song to the tune of the Westminster bell chimes. Two leaders are chosen, one named 'orange' and the other 'lemon'. They stand opposite one another and join their hands to form an arch. The children troop under one by one, singing the song. When it comes to the last line, the leaders bring down their arms on the final word, and whoever is caught then has to join either the 'orange' or the 'lemon' team and stand behind the leader. The game ends in a tug of war. A variant is that which side is 'orange' and which 'lemon' is kept secret – the child who is 'chopped' whispers which he wants to join and is allocated to the relevant side. This keeps up the suspense as to which will end up the strongest.

Oranges and lemons
Say the bells of St Clement's
You owe me five farthings
Say the bells of St Martin's
When will you pay me?
Say the bells of Old Bailey
When I grow rich
Say the bells of Shoreditch
When will that be?
Say the bells of Hackney

I'm sure I don't know
Says the Great Bell of Bow.
Here comes a candle to light you to bed
Here comes a chopper to chop off your head.
Chop, chop CHOP.

St Catherine's Day: 25 November

Catherine was an early Roman martyr who was killed, tradition says, by being tied to a spiked wheel – hence the Catherine Wheel firework. She is also the patron saint of lacemakers. This is partly again a link with the wheel – lace being a pattern of more or less a series of interconnected wheels – and the fact that she was a young girl, and lacemaking was traditionally carried out by young girls. Their eyesight was good, and the work required nimble fingers. In parts of Britain, you will find traditional lacemakers' cottages, with large windows to let in the maximum amount of light. St Catherine's Day, falling at the end of November when the days were growing dark, was a holiday for lacemakers and meant the start of a good long period when they could enjoy respite from work as the light was poor. (But think of young girls cooped up in cottages on sunny days, having to work hard at making lace when they should have been out in the fresh air . . .)

The traditional thing to eat is a Cattern Pie, an open pie filled with mincemeat (see recipe among the Christmas foods) topped with stewed apple, served with cream. The pie should have strips of pastry to make it look like a wheel, and you don't have a slice, you have a 'spoke' of Cattern Pie.

After supper, girls would tuck up their long skirts and jump over a lighted lacemakers' candle for luck!

Queen Catherine – wife of Henry VIII – who came from Aragon in Spain, popularized lacemaking in England, bringing designs from her native country, and was partly responsible for setting up the Nottingham lace industry.

Young lacemakers in Paris had a special church service and new dresses and bonnets for St Catherine's Day, and were traditionally presented with posies by gentlemen as they walked to Mass!

The tradition of St Catherine being martyred on a wheel gave rise to a tradition in some parts of Europe that wheels should not be used on this day – no spinning, no milling, no moving of things on carts. And some traditions say that St Catherine was also stabbed with a knife – so no sharpening of knives or scissors on this day, and no work done by barbers!

St Andrew: 30 November

Apostle, fisherman, martyr, brother of St Peter, and patron saint of a number of countries including Scotland. His cross is a white saltire on a blue background. He is said to have been martyred by crucifixion on a cross of this design. His relics were brought to Scotland, to the place which now bears his name and has a famous university, by St Rule (or Regulus), a Greek monk.

Traditional Scottish food is haggis, bannocks (bread rolls), whisky, shortbread, baked haddock, Dundee cake, and colcannon (mashed potato with fried cabbage and fried onion beaten into it). Any of these would be worth sampling on St Andrew's Day. Have some Scottish music, drink a toast to the memory of Bonnie Prince Charlie, or – best of all – hold a *celidh* and have an evening of excellent, lively Scottish dancing. Use CDs or tapes of traditional Scottish music. Have someone who knows the dances explain things first: many are easy to learn, and great fun to do. All ages can join in. Have cold drinks on offer for the dancers.

An old tradition says that if a girl walks barefoot to a damson tree on this day, and shakes the branches, she may hear a dog bark – and the direction from which the barking comes is the direction from which her truelove will come!

Athol Brose for St Andrew's Day

> 1¼ lb rolled oats
> 6 tablespoons whisky
> 8 tablespoons honey
> Juice of one lemon

Melt all the liquid ingredients together, mix with the porridge oats, and leave for two hours in the fridge. Fold in half a pint of whipped cream. Enjoy.

The year ends ...

And so the year ends ... as we approach Advent again and Christmas glitters on the horizon. In November, the year seems to die around us, trees shedding their leaves, daylight fading early, cold weather arriving, prayers for the dead in Church and scarlet poppy wreaths on war memorials. But Christmas with its message of new life and new hope is ahead of us, and we will recall Christ's birth and the ever-present reality of our redemption.

We are destined for Heaven – where we will all join in the 'marriage feast of the Lamb'. By fasting and feasting here on earth, we prepare ourselves for this heavenly banquet, learning the story of the Incarnation and discovering its implications. Celebrating feasts and seasons is not just something that is fun to do – it helps us to stay rooted in the truths that established our civilisation, truths that remain good news for us all and must be passed on to each new generation.

Appendix

Some books to which every child should have access:
Anne of Green Gables (and associated books) by L. M. Montgomery
Children of the New Forest by Captain Marryat
Black Beauty by Anna Sewell
Ballet Shoes, *The Bell Family*, *Wintle's Wonders*, *Apple Bough*, and other books by Noel Streatfield
Heidi by Johanna Spyri
Little House on the Prairie (and associated books) by Laura Ingalls Wilder
Little Women (and associated books) by Louisa M. Alcott
Swallows and Amazons, *Swallowdale*, *Winter Holiday*, and other books by Arthur Ransome
The Country Child by Alison Uttley
The Chalet School books by Elinor Brent Dyer
The Jungle Book by Rudyard Kipling
The Lord of the Rushie River by Cecily M. Barker
The Treasure Seekers, *The Railway Children*, and other books by E. Nesbit
Tom Sawyer by Mark Twain
Treasure Island, *Kidnapped*, *Catriona*, and other books by Robert Louis Stevenson
The Lion, the Witch and the Wardrobe and the other Narnia books, by C. S. Lewis
The Secret Garden, *A Little Princess*, and other books by Frances Hodgson Burnett
A Child's Garden of Verses by Robert Louis Stephenson
Winnie the Pooh, *The House at Pooh Corner*, and other books by A. A. Milne
The Wind in the Willows by Kenneth Graham

Older children will enjoy:
The *Father Brown* stories by G. K. Chesterton
The *Sherlock Holmes* stories by Sir Arthur Conan Doyle
The *Lord Peter Wimsey* stories by Dorothy L. Sayers

Reach for the Sky (biography of Douglas Bader) by Paul Brickhill
Edmund Campion by Evelyn Waugh
That Hideous Strength and linked books by C. S. Lewis.
Cautionary Verses by Hilaire Belloc
The *Horatio Hornblower* books by C. S. Forrester
Anne Frank's Diary
Island Magic and other books by Elizabeth Goudge
Fabiola by Cardinal Wiseman
The Lord of the Rings series by J. R. R. Tolkien
Detective stories by Agatha Christie and Ngaio Marsh

and in mid- to late teens, start them on Charles Dickens, the Brontës, and Jane Austen's novels.

Answers to Christmas Quiz

1. Oliver Cromwell.
2. Gabriel.
3. Kaspar, Melchior, and Balthasar. Their remains are said to be in the Cathedral at Cologne.
4. His symbol is three bags of gold, and these are represented by the three golden balls hung outside a traditional pawnbroker's shop. He is a patron saint of those who are poor – the sort of people who used to go to pawnbrokers.
5. King of Bohemia (in the modern-day Czech Republic), martyred by his pagan half-brother Boleslas.
6. George V.
7. 'The place of bread'.
8. Anno Domini – the Year of the Lord. We date our years from the time of Christ's birth.
9. The original name was 'Cratch cradle', referring to the crib in which Jesus was laid as a baby. The design made by the string on children's fingers is in the shape of a cradle or a manger.
10. Egypt.
11. Nazareth. Joseph was a carpenter.
12. Zachariah
13. 24 June.
14. 25 March.
15. 2 February. Presentation of Christ in the Temple.
16. 'Glory to God in the highest'.
17. Isaiah.
18. 'Coming'.
19. Third Sunday in Advent.
20. Manifestation – meaning the revealing of God to the world.
21. A doctor, a fellow-worker with St Paul.
22. Archbishop of Canterbury in the reign of Henry II, martyred on 29 December, hence the link with Christmas.
23. Early Roman martyr, a young virgin. Feast-day 13 December.
24. Gold, as he is a king. Frankincense, as he is God. Myrrh, as he will suffer for us.

Answers to Lenten Quiz

1. 'Goodbye to meat'.
2. 'Fat Tuesday' – i.e. eating up all the nice things before Lent begins on Ash Wednesday.
3. Last year's palms from Palm Sunday.
4. Thursday.
5. Two, one on either side of him.
6. Going to confession and receiving absolution.
7. It means command – from the Latin *mandatum*.
8. The ceremony in which the Queen distributes money to as many men and women as there are years of her reign – it derives from the older ceremony of washing the feet of twelve poor men.
9. Forty days.
10. Forty days.
11. Forty years.
12. Judas Iscariot.
13. St Peter.

A Note on Measurements

Some of the recipes in this book are in pounds and ounces. Younger readers will be more familiar with metric measurements, whereas North American readers use cups. Here is a table of basic measurements as a rough guide:

WEIGHTS

Metric	Imperial	American
25 gr	1 oz	
50 gr	2 oz	
125 gr	4 oz	1 cup (flour)
225 gr	8 oz	1 cup (sugar or fat)
500 gr	16 oz (1lb)	

LIQUID MEASURES

125 ml	¼ pint	½ cup
250 ml	½ pint	1 cup
500 ml	1 pint	2 cups

Pater Noster
Some recipes call for something to be done 'for the space of one *Pater*'. This refers to the *Our Father*, said in Latin, and here it is:

Pater Noster, qui es in caelis, sanctificeture nomen tuum. Adveniat regnum tuum, fiat voluntas tuas, sicut in caelo et in terra. Panem nostrum cotidianum da nobis hodie; et dimitte nobis debita nostra sicut et nos dimittimus debitoribus nostris; et ne nos inducas in tentationem; sed libera nos a malo.

Amen